D0201186

Titleist

GOLF'S LAST SECRET FINALLY REVEALED

JOHN NOVOSEL WITH
JOHN GARRITY

DOUBLEDAY
New York London Toronto Sydney Auckland

PUBLISHED BY DOUBLEDAY
a division of Random House, Inc.

DOUBLEDAY and the portrayal of an anchor with a dolphin are registered trademarks of Random House, Inc.
1745 Broadway, New York, NY 10019

Photo credits—Tiger Woods (p. ii) by Mike Harrison. All other photographs, illustrations, and film frames by John Novosel, except the following by John Garrity: Tiger Woods (p. 6); Nick Price (p. 18); Tiger Woods (p. 19); Rich Beem (p. 19); Sergio Garcia (p. 19); Jim Furyk (p. 20); Retief Goosen (p. 46); Jose Maria Olazabal (p. 47); Tiger Woods (p. 86).

Library of Congress Cataloging-in-Publication Data

Novosel, John.
Tour tempo : golf's last secret finally revealed / by John Novosel with John Garrity. — 1st ed.
p. cm.
1. Swing (Golf) I. Garrity, John. II. Title.
GV979.S9N68 2004
796.352'3—dc22 2003067434

ISBN 0-385-50927-8

PRINTED IN THE UNITED STATES OF AMERICA
May 2004

First Edition

20 19 18 17 16 15 14 13

I have always taken a special interest in the art and science of athletic movement, so I would like to express my gratitude to all those who have taught me in person or through their writings. I am particularly indebted to three friends—Ben Jackson of Stonington, Connecticut, Gerald McCullagh of Minneapolis, Minnesota, and John Rhodes of Fort Worth, Texas. This book is dedicated to these three great teachers, whose more than one hundred years of experience in helping golfers improve and enjoy the game is the foundation for the Tour Tempo program.

I also dedicate this book to my son and personal golf guru, John Novosel, Jr. Thank you, John, for your assistance, advice, and encouragement during the development of this book.

Contents

Introduction

by John Garrity

"No one ever swung a golf club too slowly," wrote the great Bobby Jones.

Unfortunately, he was wrong. The great golfers have always swung more quickly and aggressively than middle and high handicappers. If you don't believe me, take a stopwatch and time a typical tour player's swing from takeaway to impact. The elapsed time will be between .93 seconds and 1.20 seconds, or about as long as it takes to flip a pancake. Jones, the greatest player of his time, took only 1.17 seconds to hit the ball. That's just a hair slower than today's greatest player, Tiger Woods, who generates a clubhead speed of as much as 135 miles an hour in only 1.06 seconds.

Now take that same stopwatch and time the swings of your average weekend golfer—your 5-handicapper, your 15-handicapper, your can't-get-it-airborne 30-handicapper. You'll find that these nonprofessionals take anywhere from 1.3 seconds to a full 3.0 seconds to send the ball on its way.

Conclusion: Almost *everybody* swings a golf club too slowly.

Welcome to the formerly mysterious subject of tempo. I say "formerly" because John Novosel, a businessman/inventor from Leawood,

Kansas, has found the Rosetta Stone of golf, the key to consistent and powerful ball-striking. He calls it Tour Tempo.

The secret of the touring pros is their swing rhythm—sometimes described as "timing"—and it's a secret because the pros themselves don't understand it. When they shoot 65, they say, "I got into a great rhythm with my swing. I felt like I could go for every flag." When they stumble around in 74, they say, "I had no tempo today, I was just flailing."

Tour Tempo is unmistakable. Fred Couples takes a lazy-looking swing and smacks his 5-iron 200 yards. David Toms hits fairway woods as effortlessly as he hits wedges, making the same rhythmic, repeatable stroke with every club in the bag. Walk down the tee line at any PGA Tour event and you'll see that virtually every player has a smooth, powerful swing and impeccable timing.

But Tour Tempo is also an enigma. Consider this simple question: *Who has the faster swing, Greg Norman or Ernie Els?* Anybody who follows golf will instantly answer that Norman swings much faster. Els, after all, is famous for his smooth, easy swing. Novosel, however, timed their driver swings on the same hole under tournament conditions and found that Els actually has a slightly faster swing. "This is an example of how the unaided human eye can be fooled about tempo and speed in the golf swing," Novosel writes. "This also explains why there has been so much misinformation about tempo in the past."

Want to know more about tempo in the golf swing? Good luck. Since the publication in 1918 of the first photographic golf instruction book, teaching pros have tied duffers in knots with prescriptions such as "keep your head down . . . swing in a barrel . . . keep your left arm straight . . . maintain your spine angle," while bypassing entirely the quality that everyone agrees separates the good players from the bad: tempo.

Most teaching professionals can't even define tempo, although they know good tempo when they see it. "Tempo is basically the overall speed of your swing," writes David Leadbetter in his book, *Faults and*

Fixes. "Rhythm is an entity unto itself," writes LPGA Hall of Famer Mickey Wright in *Play Golf the Wright Way.* "Like death and taxes, don't question it. Just accept it." And here's what swing gurus Bob Toski and Jim Flick say about tempo in *How to Become a Complete Golfer*: "The speed with which you take the club back doesn't necessarily relate to the speed with which you bring it forward."

They're all off the mark says Novosel, who has recorded and analyzed hundreds of golf swings for this book. Tour Tempo is not a product of good swing technique; it is the principal *cause* of good swing technique. Tour Tempo is not a personal idiosyncrasy, like a fast gait or drawling speech; it is a measurable and universally constant relationship between the time it takes to swing the club to the top of the backswing and back down to the ball.

And here's the best part: Novosel can *teach* it. No one in the history of golf instruction has been able to support that claim. Thus the subtitle: *Golf's Last Secret Finally Revealed.*

Like best-selling author Dave Pelz (*The Short Game Bible, The Putting Bible*), Novosel is not a career golf pro but an outsider with a scientific bent who conducts independent research on the golf swing. He is best known as the inventor of the XLR8R® (pronounced "accelerator"), a swing aid endorsed by some of the country's top swing coaches and used by numerous PGA Tour and LPGA golfers. ("I started using the XLR8R® to hit the ball straighter," says LPGA legend Jan Stephenson. "What I didn't know was that it was going to add fifteen yards to my drive.") Novosel charges $5,000 for two days of personal instruction at his headquarters in Overland Park, Kansas, or $300 for a Tour Tempo package that includes tempo-training tapes and an illustrated manual. John Rhodes, a *GOLF Magazine* top-100 teaching pro who has taught PGA Tour stars Hal Sutton, Tom Kite, Curtis Strange, and Peter Jacobsen, says, "I've taught and researched the golf swing for forty years and have never used anything that worked like John Novosel's Tour Tempo system."

The truth is, most golf instructionals are stale knockoffs of each other, distinguishable only by the quality of their writing and illustration. *Tour Tempo* is different. Novosel's bold promise—"Golf's Last Secret Finally Revealed"—sounds like hype, but there is nothing of the charlatan or mountebank in his method. And because his theory is based on the first scientific understanding of what happens with tempo in the golf swing, *Tour Tempo* should make believers of those who greet Novosel's claims with justifiable skepticism.

Best of all, Tour Tempo is simple. Any golfer can grasp the concept in one reading, and any golfer can take his improved swing onto the golf course within days. Says Novosel, "It's the kind of method I would have liked to have had forty years ago, when I took up golf—one that immediately and dramatically improves your game."

Tour Tempo really is "Golf's Last Secret Finally Revealed."

Theory

PART ONE

1

The Mystery of Tempo

If you're a typical golfer, you own a dozen or more instruction books. The titles may vary—*The Seven Foundations of Golf, Power Golf,* and so forth—but the contents are basically the same. How to grip the club. How to address the ball. The backswing, the downswing, the follow-through. Ninety percent of golf instruction books focus on swing mechanics. The other 10 percent counsel you on the mental and metaphysical aspects of the game—probably because the pursuit of a sound swing has left you frustrated, anxious, and clinically depressed.

> Tempo is the speed at which each of us swings based on our personality and the way we are.
>
> —Peter Kessler, noted golf historian and golf commentator, Golf Channel Academy–7-24-01

This mechanics vs. mind-set dichotomy is curious, because it ignores the one quality of the golf swing that most distinguishes the touring pro from the duffer—good tempo. The swings of the tournament players look smooth and effortless, even when they generate clubhead speeds of up to 130 miles per hour. And the pros *acknowledge* that tempo is the key to their success. When they play poorly, they say, "I just couldn't find my rhythm today." When they play well, they say, "My tempo was exceptional today."

You would expect, then, to find a whole shelf in the bookstore devoted to tempo in the golf swing.

You would expect golf schools to advertise three-day workshops on "Tempo and Timing in the Golf Swing."

You would expect Tiger Woods, in his book *How I Play Golf*, to explain how he swings with perfect rhythm under the most intense pressure.

But you don't, and they don't, and he doesn't.

There are two reasons that tempo is golf's last secret.

The first reason is that neither the golf instructors nor the touring pros can explain what good tempo is. Sam Snead, whose smooth but powerful swing served as a model for generations of golfers, said that he tried to feel "oily" when he hit the ball. Al Geiberger, whose 1980 instructional, *Tempo*, written with Larry Dennis, is the only serious treatise on the subject, defines "tempo" as "the speed of your swing . . . the ingredient that ties the swing together and produces the timing that is so essential to effective ball striking."

> It took me a long time to make up my mind to write this chapter on Rhythm, and now as I sit down to begin it I am appalled by the huge gaps in my train of thought. In fact I would like another twenty years or so to think it over in, before writing about it at all.
>
> —from *On Learning Golf* by Percy Boomer, 1946, the longest continuously published golf book in print

And then you have two-time PGA Tour player of the year Nick Price, who says, "I like to feel that my hips work at about 3 to 4 miles per hour. . . . If I move them in the range of 5 to 6 miles per hour, then the shoulders, hands and clubhead lose speed dramatically. And if I throttle back to 1 to 2 miles per hour, I find that I become too arms-and-hands oriented in order to compensate for what feels like a lack of body speed. . . . I'm looking for that balance . . . not too fast and not too slow."

These descriptions of tempo are accurate, as far as they go, but they don't offer much hope to the golfer who wants to swing like Snead, Geiberger, or Price.

There is a second reason that the golf pros and swing gurus tiptoe around tempo: *They can't teach it.* In fact, conventional wisdom holds that a golfer's swing tempo is natural, immutable, and egocentric.

A comment typical of this mind-set comes from a former PGA Teacher of the Year as he described the swing of a tour pro: "To the untrained eye, Mark O'Meara's swing no doubt appears to be a thing of controlled, seamless beauty. Of course, the real beauty of Mark's swing—his almost flawless sense of tempo—can't be seen in photographs. *Then again, it can't be taught, either.*"

"There's really no right or wrong when it comes to tempo," writes a Florida teaching pro. "If you're a fast-paced person who's always on the go, a faster tempo will probably work best for you. If you're slow and easygoing, a slower tempo will serve you well."

What Is Golfing Insanity?

It's trying to improve your game by doing the same things you've done before and expecting different results.

If you're a typical mid- to high-handicapper, you beat balls on the range, read the books and magazines, watch the videos, buy those special clubs, and take lessons. And guess what? You never really improve. Handicaps haven't gotten better in twenty years, and most golfers, after playing three years, never improve. Why? Because conventional instruction ignores perhaps the most important fundamental of golf: tempo.

With no dependable and accurate way of teaching tempo, the current model of golf instruction is broken. It doesn't work.

Ben Hogan, the argument goes, was a nervous, tightly wound man; he had a very fast swing. Snead on the other hand spoke with a Virginia drawl and never seemed to be in a hurry; he made what appeared to be an unhurried pass at the ball. It follows then that "good tempo"—whatever that is—should not be achieved by trying to swing as fast as Hogan or as slowly as Snead. Your tempo is your tempo, period.

> Let me clear up the confusion many golfers have over the difference between tempo and timing. Tempo is the speed of your swing. . . . Timing is the sequence of motion, the order in which things happen during your swing. When you have good timing, the clubhead arrives at the ball traveling at peak speed and aiming straight at the target. The ball flies long and true.
>
> —from *Tempo* by Al Geiberger with Larry Dennis, 1980

When experts *do* try to teach tempo, they come at it through the back door, teaching mechanics instead. *Tempo and Timing*, an instructional video put out in 1989, shows Fred Couples hitting balls at Florida's Bay Hill Club while noted instructor John Redman watches passively, throwing in an occasional comment on the lines of, "Fred's head remains still throughout the swing." Couples, meanwhile, divulges everything he knows about tempo in just one sentence, saying, "I just try to swing as smooth as I can."

A better effort to explain tempo involved Geiberger, who starred in a 1986 videotape produced by SyberVision, an outfit specializing in personal improvement products. On the SyberVision tape, Geiberger makes swing after swing. The aspiring golfer is supposed to watch these smooth, rhythmic swings until Geiberger's tempo infuses his own swing. There is something to be said for this approach, but as humorist Fred Beck once observed, "You can watch a champion hen lay eggs, but no matter how closely you observe the hen's form you will never be able to lay a real good egg."

A few teaching pros have come tantalizingly close to cracking the code. Ernest Jones, the man who coined the phrase "paralysis by analysis," authored a pair of best-selling golf instructionals in the 1920s. "You can't divide the swing into parts and still have a swing," he wrote. To emphasize the seamless nature of the golf swing—and to promote good tempo—Jones had his pupils hit balls while he played Viennese waltzes on a phonograph. *One*-two-three, *one*-two-three, with the clubhead starting back on one, reaching the top of the swing on two, and hitting the ball on three. Jones's approach struck many as outlandish, but he was actually ahead of his time. Sam Snead, who was a pretty decent trumpet player, consciously swung to a waltz rhythm. Jimmy Demaret, a two-time Masters champ and occasional lounge singer, released a 1950s LP of "swing-to-the-music" instrumentals and vocals.

Other pros have recognized the rhythmic nature of the ideal golf swing and tried to replicate it. My good friend John Rhodes, the *GOLF Magazine* Top-100 teacher from Fort Worth, Texas, showed up one year at the PGA Merchandise Show with an electronic metronome, which he was using to help students time their swings. When I got home to Kansas City, I bought a metronome at a music store, set it up according to John's directions, and started practicing to it. Unfortunately, I saw no improvement in my ball-striking. The metronome went on the shelf.

In California meanwhile, a teaching pro named Fred Shoemaker was getting close to the secret. Shoemaker, an accomplished amateur who turned to teaching because he found tournament golf unsatisfying, had noticed a curious phenomenon. When his pupils tried to follow all the conventional rules and prescriptions—keep your head still, turn your left shoulder under your chin, load the right side, drive your

---

Nick O'Hern was at a loss to explain his great play after he shot a 10-birdie round of 65 in the third round of the 2002 Australian Masters. "Something just clicked on the range this morning," he said, "and I started hitting the ball real good."

Question: Was the mysterious something that clicked his tempo?

---

knees toward the target, let the club drop into the slot—they made cramped, awkward passes at the ball. But if he told them to forget about the ball and literally throw the club down the fairway, something marvelous happened. They instinctively made smoother, more athletic moves. In fact, their club-throwing swings, viewed on videotape, closely resembled the golf swings of more accomplished players.

"We all instinctively know how to project an object in the most efficient way possible," Shoemaker wrote in his 1996 book *Extraordinary Golf*. "In the club-throwing exercise . . . the body and arm positions change, the head and feet are in a different place, the weight is set in a new way. Everything changes, and remarkably, it all changes at once, not in the piecemeal way that most people think is the norm. Contrary to most current teaching beliefs, I have seen strong evidence for golf learning to be an all-at-once phenomenon."

Shoemaker noticed something else. When he compared videotapes of his pupils' normal swings with their club-throwing swings, he found that their backswings were measurably faster when they threw the club.

Faster?

That had to be wrong. No reputable teaching pro encouraged amateurs to swing faster. To the contrary, golf professionals have always had one piece of advice for the high handicapper: "Slow it down." Bobby Jones all but carved it on a stone tablet when he wrote, "No one ever swung a golf club too slowly." Tommy Armour, the British and U.S. Open champion of the 1920s, told his students that they should retard their downswings with a "pause at the top." More recently, instructors have preached "low and slow"—you should take the clubhead back close to the ground at a deliberate pace.

There are several reasons why teaching pros subscribe to the low-and-slow theory. For one thing, the high handicappers they teach tend to have unrhythmic, slashing swings. To the naked eye their swings look fast, even though the clubhead is traveling at only 80 or 90 miles per hour with a driver. At the same time, the tournament pro's subjective sense of his own swing is that he hits it best when he swings at less than full power. Explaining a wayward shot, the pro says, "I got a little quick." Never mind that his "slow" swing delivers the clubhead to the ball at 120 miles per hour.

But here's the biggest reason why the pros want you to swing slowly: because they are teaching swing mechanics. *Positions.* Just as a musician must practice his scales slowly before achieving speed and fluidity, the student golfer is told he must swing slowly if he is to consciously put his body in the right positions and set the club at the desired angles. This overemphasis on body positions leads to the twenty-point checklist, the "faults and fixes" paradigm, and other forms of golfing insanity. It does not, and cannot, lead to good tempo.

To sum up: The golf swing is a complex movement involving both mechanics and tempo. These two factors bear a complementary relationship to each other; change one and you affect the other. But until now, golf instructors overemphasized the mechanical aspect, ignoring tempo. Why? Because no one really knew what tempo was. And no one knew how to teach it.

Until now.

> In the following pages, we will reveal the secret of Tour Tempo and show you how it is applied in the swings of the touring pros. You will then learn, with the aid of the enclosed Tour Tempo CD, how to apply this fundamental principle to your own game.
>
> This information on tempo has never appeared in any published book or article, but golfers who have trained in our pilot tempo-training programs have achieved spectacular results. Purchasers of our Tour Tempo system typically gain from 10 to 40 yards, instantly, with every club in the bag. This increase in distance, combined with measurable improvements in accuracy, have allowed Tour Tempo students to reduce their handicaps by 50 to 80 percent in one season.

"The most exciting phrase to hear in science, the one that heralds new discoveries, is not 'Eureka!' (I have found it) – but *'That's funny . . .'*"

Isaac Asimov, author of over 500 books and possibly the most famous science fiction writer of all time

2

Breaking the Code

Some of the world's greatest discoveries have been accidental. Henri Becquerel discovered radiation when he put uranium crystals in a drawer with some photographic plates. Archimedes gained his famous insight into the displacement of fluids while taking a bath. Isaac Newton, we are told, made an intuitive leap toward understanding gravity when an apple fell on his head.

The discovery of a mathematical constant in the golf swings of the touring pros may not be as important as those breakthroughs—to nongolfers, anyway—but it, too, was a product of serendipity.

The precipitating event took place one morning in the summer of 2000, when I was editing videotape for a golf infomercial at my home studio in Leawood, Kansas. The tape was a swing sequence of LPGA star Jan Stephenson, shot a few days before in Minneapolis on the practice range of the Rush Creek Golf Academy. Jan was hitting her driver and hitting it beautifully; the swing I was reviewing had sent the ball over 250 yards to the opposite end of the range. I ran the tape back and forth on our editing equipment, frame by frame, studying the positions Jan was in at various points in her swing.

For no particular reason, I looked at the digital frame counter, which in Apple's Final Cut Pro software appears in a little box above and to the right of the image. (Broadcast video is composed of 30 images per second, so an individual frame occupies the screen for about 33 thousandths of a second. Each frame has a specific "address" measured in minutes, seconds, and frames. As the clubhead makes its first move on the backswing, for instance, the counter might read 0:14.27, meaning 14 seconds and 27 frames.)

> I think that most of us overrate the value of good mechanics in golf and underrate the value of accurate timing.
>
> —from *On Learning Golf* by Percy Boomer

Clicking the mouse to advance Jan's driver swing frame by frame, I noticed that she took 27 frames to get from the start of her swing to the top of her backswing. Nine more frames elapsed before the club arrived at the ball.

A 3-to-1 ratio.

I may have yawned. The conventional wisdom on tempo in the golf swing was that each golfer has his or her own individual tempo. If you are a fast walker and a fast talker, you were supposed to swing fast. If you are a slow walker and a slow talker, you would naturally swing slowly. (Whatever *fast* and *slow* meant. There is no quantifiable standard meaning for those terms.) I made a mental note of Jan's numbers and continued working.

> We have 14 clubs in our bags, but we only need one swing.
>
> —Jack Nicklaus

A few hours later I began studying the swing of one Eldrick "Tiger" Woods. We had a tape of the 1997 Masters, which Tiger had won by a tournament-record 12 strokes. I found myself looking intently at Tiger hitting an 8-iron approach shot. Running the video frame by frame, as I had with Jan, I noticed something strange. Tiger's 8-iron swing took 1.2 seconds from takeaway to impact, the same as Jan's driver swing. And just like Jan, he took 27 frames to get to the top of his backswing and another 9 frames to get back down to the ball.

This time, I definitely did not yawn.

In the summer of 2000, I started taping the television coverage of PGA Tour events for analysis in my studio. After studying the swings of numerous players, I quickly discarded the idea that 1.2 seconds was a standard swing speed for the top golfers. Nick Price, an aggressive swinger, took only .93 seconds from takeaway to impact. Mark Calcavecchia took 1.06 seconds. Bernhard Langer, a notoriously slow player, swung at a surprisingly brisk .933 seconds—shattering the conventional wisdom that swing tempo follows temperament.

But while the total elapsed time of the pros' swings showed some variation, a very clear pattern emerged when I counted the frames. Darren Clarke and Jeff Maggert took 21 frames to reach the tops of their backswings and 7 frames to come down.

A 3-to-1 ratio.

Mike Austin, the long-drive artist and swing teacher, took 27 and 9, the same frame count as Stephenson and Woods. Phil Mickelson was 24/8. In fact, when I allowed for a one-frame differential (due to operator error and the fact that the video equipment can't get closer than 33 thousandths of a second), virtually all the pros timed out at the same 3-to-1 ratio.

> We have not only to bring the club head down through the same line time after time; we must bring it down so that the club face is square with the ball at the instant of impact—and because the path of the club head is a curve, this means that impact must be timed correctly to an infinitesimal fraction of a second in the sweep of the swing. Also the club head must be accelerating at the moment of impact.
>
> —from *On Learning Golf* by Percy Boomer

Swing Ratios of the Pros

The following table shows the three most common elapsed times and frames ratios for touring pros—21/7, 24/8, and 27/9:

Nick Price, 21/7

21/7:

Jack Nicklaus, 21/7
Gary Player, 21/7
Jeff Maggert, 21/7
Nick Price, 21/7
Cary Middlecoff, 21/7
Ben Hogan, 21/7
Arnold Palmer, 20/7
Aaron Baddeley, 21/8
Colin Montgomerie, 21/8
Thomas Bjorn, 21/8
Bernhard Langer, 22/7
Lee Westwood, 22/7
Jesper Parnevik, 21/6
Darren Clarke, 21/7
Tom Lehman, 20/7
Joe Durant, 22/7
Hank Kuehne, 21/7
Annika Sorenstam, 20/7
Jerilyn Britz, 20/7
Fulton Allem, 19/7
Billy Ray Brown, 22/7
Steve Lowery, 20/7
Steve Jones, 21/7
Craig Stadler, 21/7
Mike Souchak, 20/6
Matt Gogel, 21/7

Tiger Woods (2002), 24/8

Rich Beem, 24/8

Sergio Garcia, 25/7

24/8:

Sam Snead, 24/8
Mark Calcavecchia, 24/7
Tom Watson, 24/7
Tiger Woods (2002), 24/8
Phil Mickelson, 24/8
Greg Norman, 25/8
Byron Nelson, 23/8
Seve Ballesteros, 24/8
Padraig Harrington, 25/8
David Berganio, 26/8
Fred Couples, 25/7
John Daly, 25/8
Patty Jordan, 25/8
Harrison Frazar, 22/8
Ed Fryatt, 24/7
Vijay Singh—right-handed—24/9
Vijay Singh—left-handed—21/9
Jerry Kelly, 24/9
Skip Kendall, 25/8
Jose Maria Olazabal, 24/7
Karen Davies, 24/9
Tom Pernice, 23/7
Steve Stricker, 24/8
Rich Beem, 24/8
Justin Leonard, 23/8
Sergio Garcia, 25/7
Trevor Immelman, 23/7
Ernie Els, 24/9

Jim Furyk, 27/9

27/9:

Jim Furyk, 27/9
Suzy Whaley, 28/9
Al Geiberger, 27/9
Jan Stephenson, 27/9
Ben Crenshaw, 29/8
Mike Austin, 27/9
Tiger Woods (1997), 27/9
Billy Mayfair, 27/8
Blaine McCallister, 27/8
Loren Roberts, 28/8
Susie Redman, 27/9
Bobby Jones, 26/9
Rory Sabbatini, 28/9
Hal Sutton, 27/8
Kirk Triplett, 29/8
Bob Tway, 29/8
Grant Waite, 26/8
Fuzzy Zoeller, 28/8
David Toms, 26/9
Bob Estes, 27/10
Michelle Wie, 27/9 (August 2003)

30/10:

Se Ri Pak, 31/9
Nancy Lopez, 30/10 (rookie); present day, 50/10
Jay Haas, 30/10
Michelle Wie, 30/10 (Spring 2003)
Payne Stewart, 30/9

Contrary to conventional wisdom, the world's best players—regardless of their overall swing speeds—swung to the same, consistent standard.

The **start of the swing** is defined as the first frame where there is a discernible movement of the clubhead away from the ball. The **top of the backswing** is defined as the point in the swing where the clubhead appears motionless, neither continuing away from the ball nor starting back down toward the ball. The **start of the downswing** is defined as the first frame where the clubhead starts moving back toward the ball from the top.

We allow a 1-frame differential (33 thousandths of a second) for difficult camera angles and operator judgment. Any frame count, in other words, is "plus or minus 1 frame."

One tournament in particular convinced me that we were on to something big. The 2000 Buick Open at Michigan's Warwick Hills Golf & Country Club was won by Rocco Mediate. But Tiger Woods and Phil Mickelson were also in the field, and we put their swings under the microscope. In the second round Tiger boomed his drive on the 584-yard, par-5 seventh hole. Hitting from the fairway with his driver from 316 yards out, Woods hit a great shot that rolled onto the green. Mickelson, meanwhile, had 290 yards to the hole on the par-5 sixteenth. Like Woods, "Lefty" pulled out his driver, and like Woods he hit a brilliant shot to the front of the green. When I timed these two great swings on our equipment, I found that their frames ratio was the same—3-to-1.

Later, though, Mickelson got into trouble on the par-3 seventeenth, pulling his 185-yard tee shot over the green to the right. When I counted the frames for this wayward shot, I found that Phil's ratio was 3.5-to-1—considerably off the consistent 3-to-1 he had exhibited all day. And when I ran the video back and forth, frame by frame, I could see where Mickelson had spent those extra fractions of a second. At the top of his swing he had rerouted the club slightly. The shaft, instead of starting directly down on the path it had followed to the top, moved a few inches behind him before starting down. Viewed at full speed, the hitch was impossible to pick up, but the frame count had pointed to some deviation in Mickelson's action.

> "You can observe a lot by just watching."
>
> —Yogi Berra

I felt like the astronomer who had deduced the planet Pluto from the erratic orbit of Neptune. Conventional wisdom says that a bad shot is caused by faulty swing mechanics. Fair enough. The loose hand action that caused Mickelson to pull the ball was visible on the tape. But you could just as easily blame his bad shot on a failure of tempo. Instead of swinging at his usual, efficient 24/8, Mickelson had either slowed his backswing or delayed his forward swing, causing him to dither at the top.

Looking for other examples of mistimed swings, I reviewed my tape of the 2000 Masters. On the thirteenth hole in an early round, Tiger had pushed his drive, the ball coming to rest on a bed of pine needles underneath some trees. When I crunched the numbers, I found that his swing ratio on that drive was a pokey 3.46-to-1 instead of his usual 3-to-1.

His forward swing was fine, but his backswing was too slow, causing him to miss the fairway.

I spent the rest of the summer checking the swings of great golfers from the past. Film from the 1961 U.S. Open at Denver's Cherry Hills Country Club revealed that Arnold Palmer made his famous charge to victory with a 20/7 swing. Film from the 1946 Masters showed Ben Hogan swinging at 21/7 and the great man himself, Bobby Jones, swinging at 26/9. I was particularly excited when I found a tape of Al Geiberger in the second round of the 1977 Danny Thomas Memphis Classic. That, of course, was the day Geiberger shot the first 59 in PGA Tour history.

When we put Geiberger's swings on the computer and counted the frames, we discovered that his ratio for that day was 27/9. *Perfection.*

As we accumulated more and more data, it was impossible to escape the conclusion that for at least fifty years the world's best golfers have been swinging to a standard, specific rhythm. I decided to call this standard "Tour Tempo," because better than 95 percent of the touring pros we timed fit the model. Sam Snead and Jesper Parnevik, Cary Middlecoff and Aaron Baddeley, Byron Nelson and Thomas Bjorn—they all swung to the 3-to-1 ratio. The long-accepted view that every golfer has his or her own special swing tempo had been disproved.

What we had discovered was the fact that instead of tempo in the golf swing conforming to the individual's swing, it was just the opposite.

Start of the swing

Top of the backswing

Start of the downswing

Impact

Tempo was a universal standard in the golf swing that the individual golfer must conform to.

The data also contradicted the conventional wisdom that the pros take the club back "low and slow." A lazy backswing, by tour standards, is 27 frames (.90 seconds), and most pros take the club back in only 24 frames (.80 seconds) or 21 frames (.70 seconds). A ball dropped from shoulder height, to make a comparison that struggling golfers will understand, hits the ground in approximately 16 frames. Furthermore, certain players are "stealthy fast"—that is, they somehow manage to camouflage the speed of their swings with a fluid motion. I was stunned, for instance, when I compared the swings of Greg Norman and Ernie Els on the same tee during the 2000 International at Colorado's Castle Pines Golf Club. To the naked eye Norman's swing is faster by a bunch. *Everybody,* in fact, looks faster than Els, who got his nickname "Big Easy" because of his slow, effortless swing. But when I timed their swings on the computer, Ernie was a frame *faster* than Greg from takeaway to impact. Obviously the naked eye can be fooled about tempo and speed in the golf swing.

Fortunately, to understand tempo we no longer have to rely on the unaided eye of the observer or the subjective testimony of the golfer. By the end of the summer of 2000, I had collected enough data to conclude that Tour Tempo in the golf swing consists of two aspects.

Aspect number one is the *ratio* of (A) the elapsed time it takes a player to get to the top of the backswing from the start of the swing compared with (B) the elapsed time that it takes to get back down to impact from the start of the forward swing. This universal ratio is 3-to-1. It takes three times as long for a player to get from the start of the backswing to the top of his backswing compared to the time it takes to get from the start of the forward swing to impact. This can be expressed in frames of video as 21/7, 24/8, and 27/9.

Aspect number two is the *amount* of elapsed time, measured in hundredths of a second, that it takes the club to go from the start of the backswing to impact. Three different elapsed times correspond with the three different ratios. Ninety-three hundredths (.93) of a second corresponds to 21-to-7. One and six one-hundredths (1.06) corresponds to 24-to-8. One and twenty hundredths (1.20) corresponds to 27-to-9.

These findings, although unexpected, absolutely make good sense. To have a consistent swing like the touring pros, you have to have a consistent time frame in which that swing takes place. You also have to have a consistent time ratio between the backswing and the return to the ball.

It follows as well that a pro plays his best golf when he manages to maintain the two aspects of Tour Tempo every time he swings the club. As we've already pointed out, when a touring pro is interviewed after a great round, he usually mentions that his tempo or timing was particularly good that day. You rarely hear a pro say that his great round was attributable to his weight shift or shoulder turn being good that day.

The real question for me was what to do with this information.

My first thought, since I work with several nationally known instructors and touring professionals, was that the pros themselves were the target audience. Tour players could save hours of practice time spent fixing "swing flaws" if they knew that their swings, however different they might look, obeyed a universal law of tempo. The pros would also benefit from tempo-testing (to identify tempo problems) and tempo-training (to correct those problems).

That was my first thought. My second thought was even more exciting: Tour Tempo, if it could be taught, might be the key to immediate, dramatic improvement by recreational golfers.

"The obvious is that which is never seen until someone expresses it simply."

Christian Morgenstern, German philosopher, 1871–1914

3

Testing the Tour Tempo Theory

Any mad scientist worth his salt performs the initial experiment on himself.

A week or so after I had identified the 3-to-1 ratio in the swings of Jan Stephenson and Tiger Woods, I set up the XLR8R® in my family room, and for the first time I added a portable cassette player and a set of earphones. The tape I popped into the cassette player was homemade and consisted of nothing but computer beeps and chirps in sets of three. The tones were synchronized to the 27/9 pattern: a beep (to mark the first movement of the club away from the ball) followed .90 seconds later by a chirp (to signal the point at the top of the backswing where the club reverses direction) and then, .30 seconds later, by another chirp (to mark the desired point of impact with the ball).

I had no idea how this tour-quality rhythm would compare to my own tempo. Slower? Faster? The same? If you had asked me to guess, I would have ventured that I was a little slower than 27/9. Like most recreational players, I followed the "low and slow" mantra of the teaching pros.

Even so, I wasn't prepared for what happened when I listened to the tones through the headphones while swinging. My first reaction was, "Holy cow! That's fast!" If I started my swing on the beep, the first chirp sounded when the club was only halfway back. The second chirp sounded before I even started my forward swing.

Having established that my swing was way slower than a touring pro's, I took the next step and tried to speed up my swing to match the tones. When I did, my swing felt impossibly fast. And since I had no way of observing myself—I wasn't taping my swings with a camcorder—I assumed it looked ridiculous as well.

Conclusion: I needed some lab rats.

Fortunately, I know several. I invited three of them to my house one afternoon—a financial consultant, a manufacturer's rep, and a retired businessman. We sat on my patio, which looks out on the first fairway of the Leawood South Country Club. They sipped cool drinks and listened while I improvised a presentation about my research. I then had them take turns swinging one of my XLR8R® training clubs to the beeps and chirps on the 27/9 tape. Each of them reacted as I had—"This is *way* too fast"—but their speeded-up swings did not look too fast. In fact, the transformation was amazing. They looked smoother, stronger, more athletic—the way Fred Shoemaker's students had looked when they hurled their golf clubs down the fairway. The striker club hit the nylon impact target with a satisfying smack. Their follow-throughs were classic; they finished with their weight balanced over the left foot and their bodies facing the target.

One of the guys, a member of Leawood South, walked around the house to his car and came back with his golf bag over his shoulder. "I'm going to play a couple of holes," he said, "just take a little turn." He put on the headphones, walked out to the first fairway, and ripped a shot toward the green. Then, with a little wave, he walked off. Thirty minutes later he returned with a big smile on his face. "John," he said, "I've got to tell you. I hit the ball *so* good. Straight as could be."

That got my attention. This guy, a financial consultant in his fifties, was a slicer, a mid-handicapper who accommodated his banana ball by aiming about 40 degrees to the left of his target. When the other guests had gone, I went out on the fairway with him and watched him nuke a fairway wood onto the green. "That's unbelievable," I said. "When's the last time you hit a ball that long and that straight?"

He didn't answer. But then, he had *beep . . . chirp-chirp* playing over and over again in his head.

These early experiments were intriguing, but I was a long way from declaring that Tour Tempo was a breakthrough in golf instruction. For one thing, the improvement my subjects saw in their swings was not quantifiable. They looked better, yes, and they hit some terrific shots. But let's be honest. Your average golfer "solves" the game of golf every couple of years. If it isn't the latest titanium driver, it's the most recent tip from the Golf Channel. ("I simply lowered my right shoulder at address, and suddenly I'm hitting it twenty yards farther and much straighter!") Such gains, I knew from experience, were largely perceptual and lasted about as long as a Valentine's Day chocolate.

The most obvious shortcoming was our failure to document the subjects' improvement. To demonstrate progress we needed to start with some baseline data—i.e., an accurate reading of the players' tempos *before* they listened to the tempo tape—and then we needed to compare those numbers to the results achieved through training. It would mean something, for instance, if improved tempo produced a measurable increase in clubhead speed. We also had to prove that the tapes actually changed a player's tempo. Otherwise, we couldn't demonstrate a correlation between Tour Tempo and improved performance.

Fortunately, I had a few suitable guinea pigs—my three sons, all graduates of the University of Kansas. John Novosel, Jr., thirty-one, was director of instruction for XLR8R® Golf. Jeff Novosel, thirty, was teaching English in Tokyo. Scott Novosel, twenty-eight, had played basketball for Roy Williams at KU and was a golf instructor and personal trainer at the Tokyo American Club in Japan. All three of my boys were low-handicap golfers with powerful swings. Scott won a 1997 qualifier for the Re/Max North America Long Drive Championship with a drive of 333 yards, and Jeff, who is ambidextrous, can drive the ball over 250 yards right- or left-handed.

> You look at pros and think he or she swings the club so smoothly yet hits the ball so far. But those two things—slow swing and hit far—don't really go together. Players who hit the ball a long way have a lot of clubhead speed. It might not look as if they are swinging the club hard, but they are swinging fast. Most people don't use all the power they have in terms of the fact that *they could swing faster.*
>
> —from *No More Bad Shots* by Hank Haney, 2001

John Jr.'s tryout was the first to follow the Tour Tempo methodology. We started out on the driving range at Hallbrook Country Club in Leawood, Kansas, where I took digital videos of Junior swinging with different clubs. We also recorded his clubhead speed with a Beltronics SwingMate®, a compact radar device that provides instant digital readouts. Junior's clubhead speed with a 5-iron was an incredible 115 miles per hour, which translates to a carry of about 210 yards. His speed with the driver was 130 miles per hour, producing about 300 yards of carry.

Back in my home studio, we copied the video to a Macintosh G4 computer and started counting frames. Junior's forward swing was tour-player fast, about 8 frames from the top to impact. His backswing, though, which featured a Sergio Garcia–style "downcock" at the top, was 31 frames—a bit slow by tour standards. If our theory was correct, Junior needed to shave 7 frames off his backswing to achieve the desired 3-to-1 ratio. Or he could retard his downswing slightly (to 9 frames) and cut just 4 frames off his backswing, which would give him the classic 27/9.

We went down to my living room, which has a high ceiling. I had

Junior put on the headphones and take a few practice swings with the XLR8R® striking club. I then asked him to take some swings while listening to the 27/9 tape. "That seems really fast," he said. "I don't think I can catch up to those tones." Within minutes, however, he was swinging to the faster tempo. His clubhead speed, measured by the SwingMate®, immediately jumped by 3 to 5 miles per hour.

I recorded these swings with the minicam, and we went back upstairs to see how they compared to the "before" pictures. This time, Junior's frame count was 28/8. This seemed to be an improvement, but it was a little ambiguous. If we allowed for a 1-frame error rate on each measurement, we could say that John was 28/9, which put him just one frame off the 3-to-1 ratio. On the other hand, most of Junior's forward swings clocked at 8 frames. That suggested that his swing model might not be the 27/9 of Tiger Woods, but the 24/8 of Jack Nicklaus and Sam Snead. I was puzzled, too, by the fact that Junior did not manage any swings that were exactly 27/9, even though he had the tones to follow. "It's a little tricky to anticipate the beeps," he said. "Particularly the one at the top of the backswing."

In the days that followed, I ran the before-and-after test on a number of volunteer subjects. My son Scott, who was visiting from Japan, brought over a couple of his friends. One of them, who had a tendency to overswing, tightened up his action the minute he slipped on the headphones. Two weeks later this young man called to tell me that he had seen dramatic gains in distance with no loss of accuracy. "It's amazing," he said. "I never realized how hard it was to time my old swing."

John Jr. meanwhile had taken the 27/9 tape to the practice range. "It's really helping my ball-striking," he said. "I'm hitting it longer and straighter." He noticed as well that virtually every player he watched on the range took a longer, slower backswing than the pros. "Nobody swings it back and through with any rhythm," he says. "They don't have a free motion. Everybody takes it back real slow and then lunges at the ball."

In one interesting experiment, we tested three junior golfers, ages thirteen, twelve, and six. The thirteen-year-old, Tucker Weems, took a slower-than-molasses 66 frames to complete his backswing, and most of his shots hugged the ground. When we put him on the 27/9 tape, his jaw dropped and his eyes got real big, as if we had asked him to clean his room in 3 seconds. But Tucker, like the other kids, had no problem speeding his swing up to match the beats. In a few minutes he was swinging at 25/9. His clubhead speed with a driver immediately jumped from 82 to 90 miles per hour. That represented an increase in carry from about 190 to 208 yards.

A few days after the training session, Tucker's dad reported that his son had driven over the trees to cut the dogleg on the thirteenth hole at Lake Quivira Country Club. "Two days before," his dad said, "he wouldn't have had a chance." Tucker, playing from the front tees, was soon shooting in the high thirties for nine holes.*

We still had some work to do. John Jr. found it easy to speed up his swing with the tempo tracks, but almost impossible to match the beats exactly. "The beat at the top of the swing is particularly hard," he said. "You have to anticipate it."

He had put his finger on the problem: *reaction time.*

Organisms don't react instantly to a stimulus; there is always a delay between the registration of the stimulus and the triggering of the response. I was reminded of a scientific study undertaken some years ago by the Golf Society of Great Britain, which published a book called *The Search for the Perfect Swing.* The GSGB researchers would put a

*You might be wondering what happened to the twelve- and six-year-olds. Josh Weems, in just 15 minutes, increased his clubhead speed by 10 percent and improved his timing from 39/11 to 28/11. Two summers later, he shot 73 at a tournament in Kansas City and had several subpar 9-hole rounds at his home course. The six-year-old, Collin Weems, also instantly increased his clubhead speed by 10 percent and improved his timing from 46/11 to 34/11. Collin was the state champion for seven-year-olds in the U.S. Kids World Golf Tournament and represented Kansas in the 2002 World Tourney in Maryland.

golfer in a room and say, "Go ahead and swing. We're going to put the lights out. The instant the lights go out, we want you to alter the path of your swing." They discovered that nobody could do it. No golfer, once his swing had started back down from the top, could do anything to change his swing before impact.

For our tempo tracks to be precise, therefore, we had to enter reaction time into the equation. The number we settled on was one-fifth of a second. That was widely accepted in scientific circles as being average for humans pushing buttons or stepping on brake pedals in response to visual or aural cues. (A teenager wielding a Whack-a-Mole hammer is somewhat quicker. A senior citizen at a changing traffic signal is a bit slower.) Working again in my Final Cut Pro program, I realigned the tones. I added a fifth of a second before the first beat (takeaway) and then moved the second beat forward by a fifth of a second to signal the change of direction at the top of the swing. The third tone (impact) stayed put, since it was more of a timing target than a stimulus requiring a response.

> If you want to find the secrets of the Universe, think in terms of energy, frequency, and vibration.
>
> —Dr. Nikola Tesla, 1856–1943, Serbian-American electrical engineer and scientist. Inventor of alternating current and holder of more than 700 patents

"That's much better," John Jr. said when he tried out the new tempo tracks. "Now I can react to the tones. I don't have to anticipate them." The difference was apparent when we taped his swing with the headphones on. He could now match the beats precisely, either at 27/9 or 24/8. We saw similar results with other golfers we tested. (See "Case Studies," Chapter 10.) It is common now at the end of a Tour Tempo training session to see a student swinging so closely to 27/9 that we can put a video of his or her swing side by side with that of Al Geiberger's, and the two swings will be perfectly synchronized.

The illustration on page 34 shows Bob Walsh, our Tour Tempo student, before training. Comparing him to our model, Al Geiberger, you can see that Bob has reached the top of his backswing at frame 41, 5 frames after Al has arrived at impact.

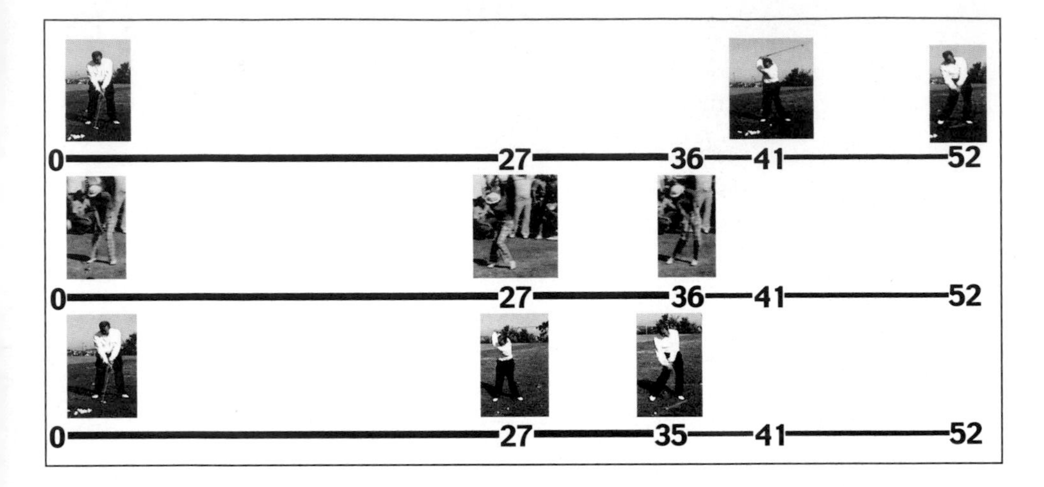

Bob Walsh, Tour Tempo student, compared with Al Geiberger before (top line) and after (bottom line) training.

Bob, after 15 minutes of Tour Tempo training, shows identical timing to Geiberger from takeaway to top of backswing and is only one frame off at impact. In less than 15 minutes, Bob increased his clubhead speed from 88 to 106 miles per hour with no loss of accuracy and better trajectory.

Another challenge was finding the right pedagogical framework for our tempo training. My initial thought—and I still lean in this direction—was that Tour Tempo is best taught over two days on a one-teacher-to-one-pupil basis. After videotaping the subject hitting balls during a round of golf, we go inside and subject his swing to computer analysis while the student watches a film explaining Tour Tempo. We then take the golfer back outside, introduce him to the Tour Tempo audio tracks, and begin the tempo training using an XLR8R® impact target and the XLR8R® striking clubs. (We believe the best way to learn a motor skill is through simulation. By creating a learning environment that closely resembles the task to be learned but with no penalties for failure, we can rid the student of the tension that inhibits correct form.) On day two, under the watchful eye of the instructor, the student begins hitting range balls to the Tour Tempo tracks. If all goes well, the training concludes in the afternoon with a playing lesson. On the golf course the pupil can practice his pre-shot routine and see how his retimed swing works under actual course conditions.

Unfortunately, only the wealthy or the obsessed can justify a pilgrimage to our headquarters in Overland Park, Kansas. To reach a wider audience we decided to merge the tempo program with our existing XLR8R® product. This new package, Tour Tempo, sells in kits ranging from $149.95 to $299.95. It includes the full XLR8R® kit (impact target, striker clubs, and resistance tails) plus our tempo-training tapes, a portable cassette player, and a detailed instruction manual.

This book, along with the attached CD, represents yet a third approach to tempo training.

Golf, it turns out, had not one but *two* last secrets to be revealed. The first, which we have examined at length, is the universal 3-to-1 tempo ratio of backswing to forward swing employed by most touring pros.

The second secret, equally important, is this: *Tempo is a fundamental.* As such, it should not be seen as a highly refined skill to be tackled only by single-digit handicappers. Tempo should be taught to beginning golfers at the same time they learn the other fundamentals of grip, stance, posture, and ball position. By learning about tempo at the outset, the novice golfer can escape the quicksand of body-position instruction and develop a more athletic, reflexive golf swing—one that does not depend upon conscious thought processes.

Percy Boomer, bless his golfer's soul, had it right a half century ago. "Too much thought about mechanics is a bad thing for anyone's game. Now the reason why golf is so difficult is that you have to learn it and play it *through your senses*," he wrote, "you must *feel* what you have to do."

To begin learning the feel of Tour Tempo, turn the page.

Practice

Part Two

"Eons of manhours are lost trying to substitute *effort* for *technique* and trying to eliminate *effect* instead of *cause*."

Homer Kelley, *The Golfing Machine*

4

A New Approach

Some pages back, I used the word "paradigm" and stated that the current model for learning the golf swing was "broken."

I want to elaborate on that.

In his book *Paradigms,* Joel Barker defines a paradigm as a "set of rules and regulations (written or unwritten) that does two things: (1) it establishes or defines boundaries; and (2) it tells you how to behave inside the boundaries in order to be successful."

The paradigm for learning the golf swing—I call it "Conventional Golf Wisdom" (CGW for short)—goes like this:

A The student hits balls on the range.

B The instructor watches and, when possible, records the student's swing with a video camera.

C The instructor determines what is "wrong" with the student's swing—some aspect of that last particular swing that needs fixing (the movement of the right elbow, the weight shift, the shoulder turn, etc.).

D The instructor offers remedies based on his or her particular theory of the golf swing. These remedies usually require the student to consciously change a position of the body while it is moving an object (the club) at over 100 miles per hour.

This type of instruction, with its overemphasis on body positions and conscious control of the anatomy, asks the student to "connect the dots." That leads, in turn, to the **twenty-point checklist**—the list of things your instructor wants you to check off as you perform the full swing:

A Shift your weight
B then turn your hips
C and then raise your hands
D and then drop your arms
E and then clear your hips
F and then fire your right side
G and then shift your weight laterally . . .

This approach is neither physiologically nor psychologically sound. For one thing, these positions of the anatomy are merely the effects of a good swing, not the cause. For another, they can't be consciously controlled in the time between takeaway and impact, which is little more than a second.

> The fault with much golf teaching today, professional and amateur, is that the teacher tries to eradicate specific faults by issuing specific instructions.
>
> —from *On Learning Golf* by Percy Boomer

This approach, however, has been the dominant teaching paradigm of our times and has fostered such actual book titles as *40 Common Errors in Golf and How to Correct Them; How to Correct the 80 Most Common Problems in Golf; 101 Drills to Improve Your Golf Game;*

300 Golf Solutions; and, finally, *365 One-Minute Golf Lessons*. Whoa!

You've probably become acquainted with this "faults and fixes" mentality from your own experience with golf lessons and instruction books. It sank in for a friend of mine when he joined a new golf club in Arizona and signed up for the inaugural round. He wasn't hitting the ball too well and didn't want to be embarrassed, so he decided to prepare by first taking a lesson from the teaching pro at his home club. The pro detected something wrong in his backswing, so he told my friend, "Point your left elbow out to the right as you take the club back." My friend immediately started hitting the ball better. Both he and the pro walked off the range feeling pretty good about his progress.

> To me, golf is 90 percent physical. Mentally I am very strong. How do you explain that my best score is 97?
>
> —Lama Kunga Rinpoche of Tibet, Buddhist teacher and novice golfer, upon being told that golf is mostly mental and that he should visualize his shots, a simple hint that didn't help him at all

So how did my friend do in the inaugural round? He concentrated on his elbow, just as he was told, and he quit counting lost balls after the first dozen.

I tell this story so you will understand that our system is different, "outside the box." With the Tour Tempo system you will learn the *feel* of an effective, powerful swing, not the theory behind it. If you are a low- to mid-handicapper with reasonably sound swing fundamentals, the tempo training alone will immediately take you to a higher performance level. You will never have to "work" on your full swing again. You won't have to worry about what starts your backswing, where you are at the top, or what triggers your forward swing. Those things will happen instinctively, reflexively—as they do in the swings of the pros.

If you do not already have sound swing mechanics—and let's face it, most recreational golfers are lacking in this area—don't despair. We will give you two simple drills—the Y drill and the L drill—that will teach you the most important mechanical movements in the golf swing. These drills cover all the complexities of the grooved swing—

proper swing plane, the blending of the arm swing with the body turn, achieving square impact, etc.—and can be combined with the tempo training to speed your progress.

Principles (fundamentals) are simple, yet powerful models that help us understand how the world works. Principles generate the same result each and every time—no matter where, when, or who uses them. Principles work when you work them. Gravity is a principle. When you wake up in the morning, you don't have to question which way your foot will go when you get out of bed. It goes down, never up. Likewise, two times two always equals four. It never equals five. Principles don't wear out, rust out, or give out. They last forever. They are timeless and tireless. Principles cannot be overused. Life is the process of discovering principles—of discovering what works. If you want to make rapid progress, don't fight against principles—flow with them.

—*The One Minute Millionaire* by Mark Hansen and Robert Allen

Exactly how to perform these drills is spelled out in the remaining chapters, and in the CD video film clips you will learn how to combine them in a precise step-by-step manner that we call the Tour Tempo Workout. The workout has proven to be the most effective way to train for the Tour Tempo system. *For the first time in the history of golf, the basic fundamentals of mechanics and the basic fundamentals of tempo have been combined into one simple workout.*

It can be done just about anywhere and anytime, in about 15 minutes. We show it being done at a range, but of course most of us don't have the time to take out of our daily schedules to drive back and forth to a range, or we don't go out if it's too cold or too hot or raining or snowing. So we show you how you can do the workout basically anywhere you can stand up—in your garage, basement, backyard, or office.

The Y and L drills will also tell you if you make the one disastrous swing movement that is responsible for most bad golf shots—the over-the-top "casting" motion. If you are casting, we can take care of that, too—either through tempo training alone or by using a combination of tempo training and an inexpensive swing aid.

Traditionalists may find our approach radical, if they think that it's radical to practice the basics, but there is nothing extreme or wacky about Tour Tempo. To swing like a touring pro and to hit the ball like a touring pro, you must: (1) swing the club with (2) a tour pro's tempo to achieve (3) the correct release with (4) clubhead speed and (5) square impact. These are the five fundamental aspects of the golf swing.

All reputable teaching pros believe in the importance of these five fundamentals. The principal difference in their approach and ours is this: They teach only four of the five.

We teach all five.

"They [fundamentals] are really the basic building blocks or principles that make everything work. I don't care what you're doing or what you're trying to accomplish; you can't skip fundamentals if you want to be the best."

Michael Jordan in his book,
I Can't Accept Not Trying

5

Learn Two Drills and Forget Mechanics Forever

First, an admission: Tempo isn't everything.

Tour Tempo *is* golf's last secret—I've called it the Rosetta Stone of golf—but I'll be the first to admit that good tempo alone won't produce tour-quality golf shots. Tour-quality golf shots also feature simple swing movements that enhance the pros' ability to consistently repeat the correct tempo. This *combination* is the key to consistently good golf shots. If you're lacking in this area, and most of the amateur swings we've seen are, then you must learn the basic mechanical techniques employed by most tour players.

Fortunately, you can learn the pros' swing techniques by mastering just two drills, the Y and L drills. I learned these drills from my friend John Rhodes, who has taught Hal Sutton, Tom Kite, Curtis Strange,

Peter Jacobsen, and many other touring pros. John was a friend of Ben Hogan's and learned from Ben what was then called the "Hogan training drill." John modified the Hogan drill and broke it down into the Y and L drills. I have further changed some of the positions in the drill to make it conform better to the modern golf swing.

Once you've mastered the Y and L drills, you can say good-bye to swing mechanics once and for all. And here's more good news: Once you've learned these drills, you'll be able to play 95 percent of your golf shots with the same motion. The feel that you develop with the Y drill is perfect for chip shots and short bump-and-run shots.

Retief Goosen chipping with the Y drill

The L drill is excellent for knockdown-type approach shots where accuracy is paramount. The L drill also gives you the tools to spin the ball and back it up next to the pin.

Best of all, the Y and L drills are perfect for practicing to the Tour Tempo audio tracks. They also form the basis of the Tour Tempo Workout, which is fully described on the CD. The workout is our preferred way of incorporating everything you need to learn about tempo and mechanics into your golf swing.

Jose Maria Olazabal on the course with the L drill

In the workout, you'll notice that we first *walk-through* the mechanical movements of each drill while brushing the grass. Once we achieve the proper technique while doing this, we then advance to walking through the movements and actually hit the ball with the *walk-through* motions. Once these are satisfactorily completed, then we combine the walk-through movements with the correct tempo in seamless movement to the tones.

In the following pages, you will learn how to master these drills.

The Y Drill

The Y formed by club, arms, and shoulders

The "Y" in the Y drill is formed by your club, arms, and shoulders when you address the ball. Your goal in the Y drill is to retain the Y while swinging the club back to the level of your waist and then forward again to a low finish. Maintaining the Y in this fashion gives structure to your setup and encourages a one-piece takeaway.

Your club, arms, and shoulders form a Y at (1), the address position.

Maintain the structure of that Y as you move the club back to position (2), the top of the backswing for Y Drill. The Y will not be perfect when you get to this position, but do the best you can.

From (2), set the wrists* (2A) and swing the club through (3), the

* "Setting" the wrists is explained at the end of the Tour Tempo workout video on the CD.

impact position, to (4), the finish. Notice that the Y formed by the arms and shaft have been retained.

This drill looks simple and *is* simple, but it won't work its magic unless you get the position of the club right in three dimensions. For example, at (2) the club shaft must be parallel both to the line of flight and to the ground, and the leading edge of the clubface should be perpendicular to the ground. The grip end of the club should be just outside and above your right foot.

To start with, just walk through the Y drill in slow motion, acquainting yourself with the correct positions of the club. Stop at (2) and take a look at the club. Then swing slowly through impact to the finish. *It is important that the club ends up exactly as shown.*

Once you have mastered these positions, go ahead and complete the Y drill by swinging the club in one continuous motion. The following pages will elaborate on the Y drill.

1. Address

2. Top of backswing for Y drill

2A. Set

3. Impact

4. Finish

Three photos of position (2), top of backswing, view from behind:

Incorrect. The club shaft is neither parallel to the ground nor parallel to the target line.

Correct. The club shaft is about parallel to the ground and about parallel to the target line.

Incorrect. The club shaft is parallel to the ground, but not parallel to the target line.

Biomechanical stick-figure graphics of position (2) showing belt-buckle view, view from behind, and view from above:

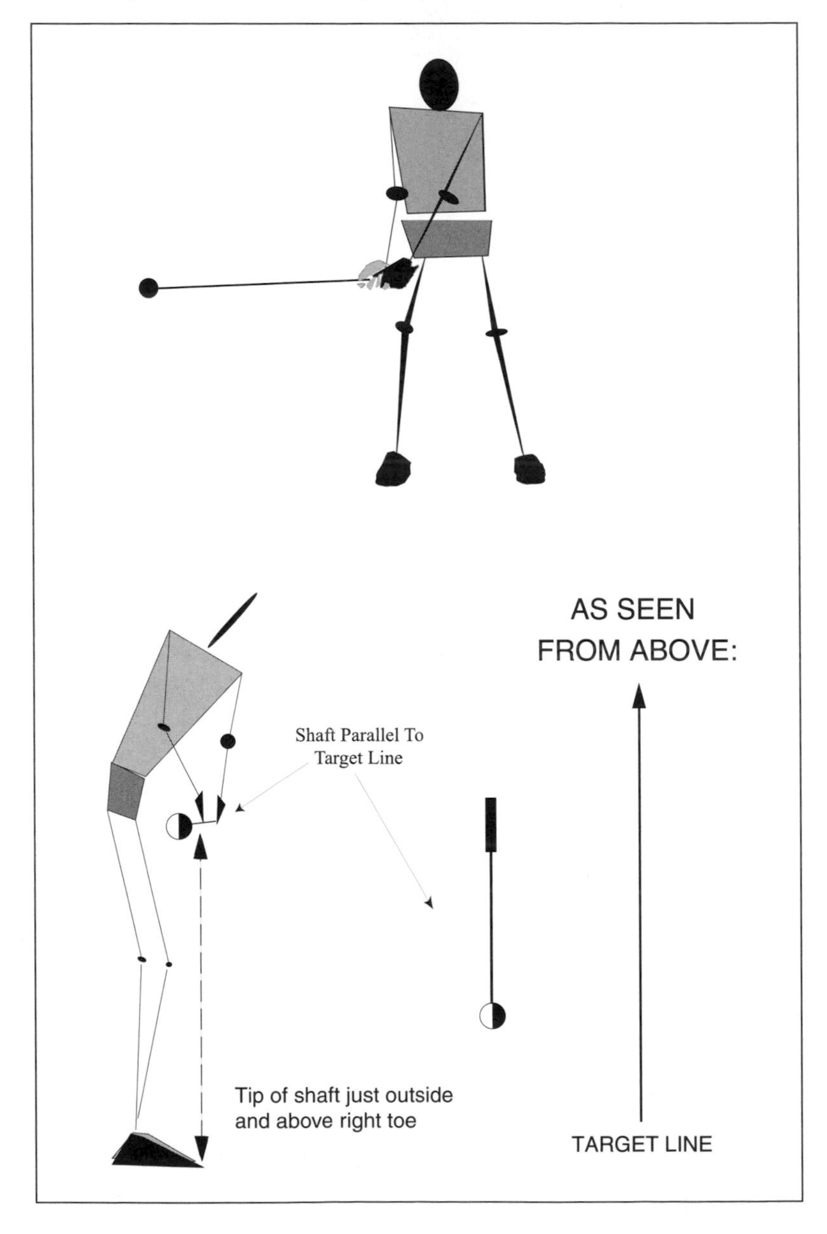

The three dimensions of position (4), the finish:

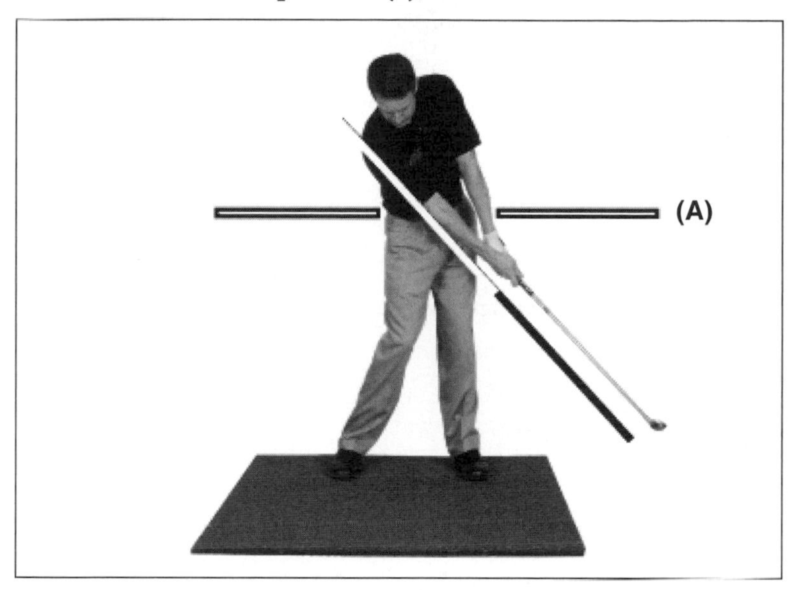

Dimension 1. Club shaft 30 to 40 degrees below a line (A) that would run parallel to the ground, with the end of the grip as its fulcrum point.

Dimension 2. Clubhead end of shaft pointing to target line. If you were looking at the face of a clock, the shaft would be pointing to about 4:30.

Dimension 3. Grip below waist high.

"What kind of golf swing am I learning with these drills?"

Answer: The modern swing.

Today's tour players swing "tight and wide"—that is, they make a shorter backswing with more extension away from and through the ball. This modern swing is more repeatable and less susceptible to error than the "armsy" swing favored by tour players of the seventies and eighties. It allows players to control the ball better while hitting it farther. It gives tour players the ultimate mix of repeatability, accuracy, and distance.

You can learn the modern swing, too . . . by combining the Y and L drills with the Tour Tempo audio tracks.

The L Drill

The L drill starts exactly like the Y drill. You just add about 45 degrees to the backswing and 45 degrees to the finish. The club shaft, which in the Y drill was parallel to the ground at position (2), top of the backswing, now points down at the target line.

The "L" is formed by the leading forearm and the club shaft.

The backswing is the same as in the Y drill, but about 45 degrees longer.

The finish is the same as in the Y drill, but about 45 degrees longer.

Five-photo sequence of the L drill:

1. Address

2. Top of backswing

2A. Set

3. Impact

4. Finish

The three dimensions of position (2), top of the backswing:

Dimension 1. Club shaft points to target line.

Dimension 2. Shaft is 5 to 10 degrees short of being perpendicular to the ground.

Dimension 3. Grip between waist and armpit.

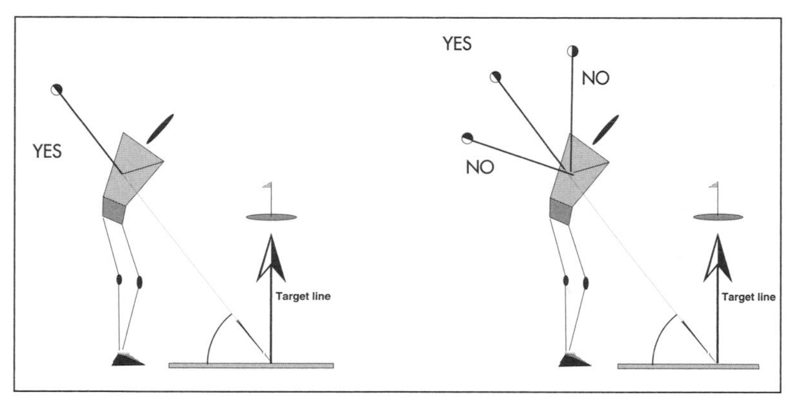

Incorrect. The end of the grip points inside the target line.
Incorrect. The end of the grip points outside the target line.
Correct. The end of the grip points at the target line (as pictured below).

The three dimensions of position (4), the Finish:

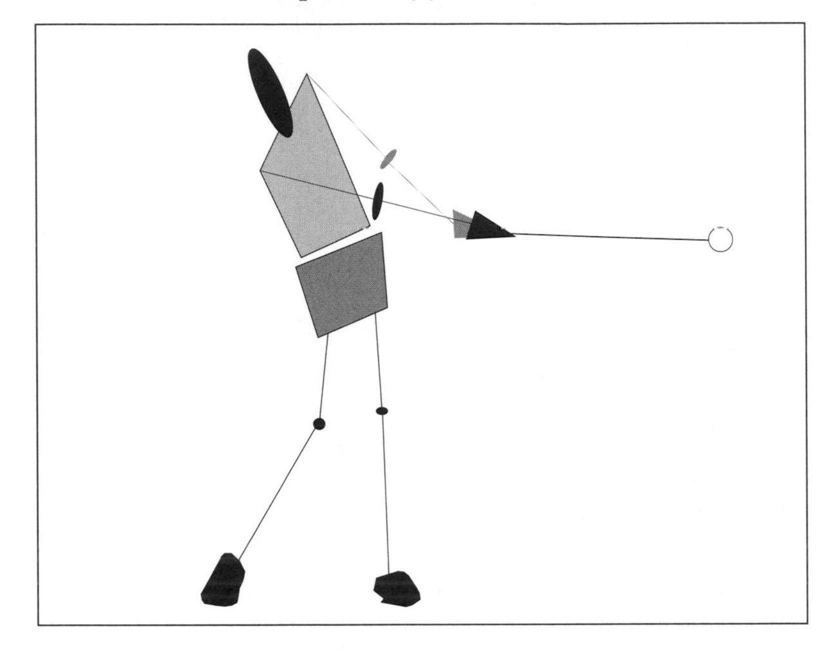

Dimension 1. Club shaft approximately parallel to target line.
Dimension 2. Shaft short of being parallel to ground.
Dimension 3. Grip about waist high.

Here again, we are going to ask you to become an expert at these drills. Your mastery of the golf swing will be determined by how well you learn them.

Why It's Best to Practice without a Golf Ball

Conventional instruction has you performing drills with golf balls. This seems logical, but when you hit balls, you become more interested in proper ball flight than in acquiring a feeling for swing movement. Learning studies have proven that there is a better way to learn most motor skills: simulation. With simulation, you create a learning environment that corresponds as closely as possible to the task to be learned, with no penalties for failure.

For this reason, we recommend that you begin the Y and L drills without a ball. The model in the photograph is practicing with our proprietary training device, the XLR8R® (pronounced "accelerator"). It combines a fabric impact target with a naturally weighted striking club, allowing the student to feel the correct swing form without worrying about ball flight. The XLR8R® is particularly good for drills and tempo training because the Velcro interfaces of the striking club and target provide accurate feedback on swing plane, clubhead path, and squareness of impact.

1. Address

2. Top of backswing

3. Finish

The XLR8R®

"We will simplify the things you have to learn by stringing them together into cycles of sensation because they are then easier to remember."

Percy Boomer,
On Learning Golf

6

Getting Started

It's time to put to use what we've learned about tempo. Get out your Tour Tempo CD and insert it in a portable disc player or computer. (A CD Walkman with 45 seconds or more of skip protection is ideal; you can wear it on your belt and listen through headphones as you swing the club.) Take a golf club that you feel comfortable with—a 7-iron is a good choice—and find a quiet, secluded place where you can swing. You aren't going to hit golf balls yet, so your backyard is fine. So is your den, if you have a high ceiling and a rug you're thinking of replacing.

Setting the CD player at a comfortable volume, select **27/9 Pre-shot**. You will hear a series of repetitive tones—a dull chime followed by two high-pitched beeps. You are already familiar with these tones if you watched the video segments on the Tour Tempo CD. The low tone corresponds to the takeaway of the golf club from the address position. The two beeps correspond to the top of the backswing and impact, respectively.

27/9 Pre-shot is programmed at 27/9, the slowest of the three Tour Tempo ratios. This is the swing speed employed by Al Geiberger, Bobby Jones, and Jan Stephenson.

24/8 Pre-shot is programmed with beats timed at 24/8. This is the swing speed employed by Phil Mickelson, Sam Snead, Tom Watson, and, since about 1999, Tiger Woods.

21/7 Pre-shot is programmed with beats timed at 21/7. This is the swing speed employed by Ben Hogan, Nick Price, Gary Player, and Darren Clarke.

Each audio band will play for 3 minutes before stopping. If your CD player has a REPEAT mode, you can make the band play over and over again in an endless loop.

The first step is to see how your swing compares to the swings of the touring pros. Make a practice swing while listening to the tones on Audio Band 1.

- Start your backswing on the first beat, the low-pitched tone.
- The second beat, a beep, is your cue to start swinging down to impact.
- The third tone, another beep, corresponds to impact. Try to time your forward swing so that impact and the beep are simultaneous.
- Make sure that all your movements are smooth, not jerky.
- **Do not anticipate the first and second beats. Just react to them with the appropriate action.**

If you are like most golfers we have tested, your first impression will be: "The tones are too fast. I can't swing that fast. *Nobody* can swing that fast!"

This is normal. You have probably been making an exaggeratedly slow backswing most of your life. To you the tour player's tempo—even this relatively slow 27/9—will feel like the *swish-swish* of Zorro's sword.

In fact, your forward swing with the tones will probably not be much, if any, faster than it was before. The difference is in the backswing. Touring pros take the club back quickly and efficiently. They don't waste time with swing-path detours or counterproductive "positionings" of the club or body.

> The soundest and most permanently profitable motions in golf feel unnatural and "all wrong" to most people when first tried.
>
> —Percy Boomer, *On Learning Golf*

Tour Tempo feels fast at first because it *is* fast.

Now, just to get a feel for the 3-to-1 ratio that is the basis of Tour Tempo, select **21/7 Pre-shot** on the CD. This is the 21/7 tempo. While listening to the tones, take a few short swings that approximate chip shots. As before, start the club back when you hear the low-pitched first beat; start your downswing on the second beat; brush the grass with the club on the third beat. You may find it hard to believe, but Ben Hogan hit his driver at this tempo.

"Brush the Grass" as shown on the CD

1. Address

2. Top of backswing

3. Impact

4. Finish

Switch to **24/8 Pre-shot**, the 24/8 tempo. This time, try to match the beats while making a pitch-shot swing with a wedge. (And consider this: Tiger Woods, without benefit of tones or any other external timing device, matches this tempo virtually every time he swings his wedge, whether it's on the practice range or the golf course.)

Finally, return to **27/9** and make some more swings to the beats of 27/9.

The Tour Tempo audio tracks have a clear purpose. They establish the intrinsic tempo of the golf swing in your subconscious mind. Once this is accomplished, you will not have to think about tempo while playing. It will be internalized.

This is what the touring pros have already done. At some point in their lives, whether by intuition or by accident, they discovered the correct tempo of the golf swing and practiced it until it was stored in their internal clocks. That's why the pros are such consistent ball-strikers. They know how to apply their correctly programmed inner clocks to the golf swing.

You are about to acquire that same ability.

The Swing-Set Drill

We have found the best way to get used to the Tour Tempo program is to first practice aspect number one—takeaway to top of backswing. Start your swing on the first tone and swing back until your hands are as high as your armpits. Do this over and over, until you feel the proper speed with which to take back the club in order to arrive at this position on the second tone. You can also do this with the Y Drill, and you will notice that the swing back requires a relatively slower speed than the L Drill. The Swing-Set Drill is more fully explained in the Tempo Testing video on the CD.

The Swing-Set Drill (continued)

1. Establish where you want your backswing to end. In the accompanying illustration, it would end when the hands reach shoulder height.

2. Get in your address position and listen for the first tone. Upon hearing the first tone, swing the club back as you normally would.

The Swing-Set Drill (continued)

3. Make a mental note of where the second tone sounds as you go back. In this case, the player is only halfway to the top. The backswing is too slow by Tour Tempo standards.

4. To correct your tempo, start the club back on the first tone and try to sync the second tone with the desired top-of-backswing position. Do not go to impact! Repeat the backswing again and again from address, syncing it with the tones.

First tone and second tone

“Everything should be made as simple as possible,
but not simpler.”

Albert Einstein

7

Programming Your Internal Clock

Now that you are familiar with the Y and L drills, let's start some actual training with the Tour Tempo CD. We will begin with the Y drill and the 21/7 audio track. We will then move on to the L drill and the 24/8 audio track. Finally, we will train your full swing with the 27/9 audio track.

Later, when you have become familiar with the tracks and drills, you can pick the Tour Tempo that you like best. But remember: No matter which Tour Tempo you ultimately choose, it is beneficial to vary the audio tracks so that you get used to the all-important 3-to-1 ratio.

Once again, take a 7-iron or the club you are most comfortable with . . .

- Insert the Tour Tempo CD in your portable player. (If you are wearing headphones with a CD Walkman, hook the player on your belt behind you and let the cord trail down your back so it won't interfere with your swing.)

- Play **21/7 Pre-shot**. This is the 21/7 track, the fastest of the three Tour Tempos.
- Start your practice session with the Y drill (or a swing that approximates a chip shot).
- Address the ball or impact target and try to match your swing to the three beats. The first beat is your cue to start the backswing. The second beat is your cue to start swinging forward to impact. The third beat, if you time your swing correctly, will match the sound of impact.
- Make sure that all your movements are smooth, not jerky.
- Do not anticipate the first and second beats. Just react to them with the appropriate action.

The 21/7 Tour Tempo Track with the Y Drill

1. Address

Address the ball or impact target and match your swing to the three beats. On the first beat, which has a distinctly different sound from the second and third beats, start your backswing. Make sure that you take the club back smoothly. Do not anticipate the first beat. (The audio track has been programmed to allow for human reaction time, which is approximately one-fifth of a second.) As soon as you hear it, start the clubhead back.

2. Top of backswing

Does Tour Tempo still seem fast to you? Our teachers have observed that most amateurs take the club back way too slowly. The touring pros just don't do this. They are much quicker on the backswing and almost always in sync with the Tour Tempo protocol.

Here's the good news: With Tour Tempo, anytime your swing gets out of sync, you can get out the Tour Tempo CD and reprogram your internal clock.

2A. Setting the wrists

The second beat is your cue to start the club swinging back to the ball or impact target—that is, you react to the second tone (2) by setting the wrists (2A) and returning the club to the ball at impact. **Your club should still be moving backward when you hear the second beat.**

(You will notice that there isn't much time between the second and third beats—less than three-tenths of a second. That's why we recommend the XLR8R® tools for Tour Tempo training. They allow you to concentrate on the beats without worrying about ball flight.)

Do not anticipate the second beat.

When you hear the second beat, set your wrists and start the forward swing. This is a Y drill, so position (2), top of backswing, should be somewhere in the neighborhood of these two pictures. The club is changing directions, so there will be a slight lag as you do this (represented by pictures 2 and 2A). If you have been practicing the Y drill, position (2) should be keyed into your memory by now. You should not have to consciously think about it.

3. Impact

4. Finish position

The last step is to time the sound of the third beat with the sound of impact (3). It's best to concentrate on the first and second beats at first, but once you've got them down, you can concentrate on making the sound of impact occur simultaneously with the third beat.

When you have timed your impact with the third beat and are in your finish, hold that finish position (4) in a **freeze frame** until you hear the first beat of the new series.

How long should you practice to the Tour Tempo tones? You're the best judge of that, but we don't recommend that you beat balls for hours with the headphones on. When you feel your concentration waning, turn off the CD player and let your reprogrammed internal clock take over.

Quick-Start Option

Many of us like to learn new things without reading the manual. That's fine, but if you jump into Tour Tempo without first testing the waters with your toe, you may get a shock. ("I can't do it! It's too fast!") When we introduced our test subjects to Tour Tempo, we started them out with a half measure. It's called the preset drill, and it makes it easier for the golfer to transition to the new swing.

1. Preset position

2. Second tone

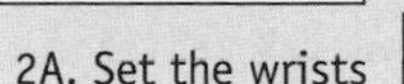

2A. Set the wrists

3. Impact

A. Start with the club in a "preset" position. That is, take your normal address and then move the club to (1). The grip should be approximately in front of your back foot. The shaft should be parallel to your target line, the toe of the club pointing up.

B. When you hear the first tone (1), start the club backward and upward until you hear the second tone. React to the second tone by setting the wrists (2A) and returning the clubhead to the ball at impact. The sound and feel of impact and the third tone (3) should occur simultaneously.

Everybody we work with quickly gets accustomed to the tones, and we usually have them swinging from a normal address position within 10 or 15 minutes. We have found that it is best to initially tee up the ball when using this and the other drills.

The 24/8 Tour Tempo Track with the L Drill

1. Address

As in the previous drill, address the ball or impact target and match your swing to the three beats of **24/8 Pre-shot**, the 24/8 track. Your lead arm in the L-drill swing, remember, goes back about 45 degrees farther than it does in the Y-drill swing.

On the first beat, which has a distinctly different sound from the second and third beats, start your backswing. Make sure that you take the club back smoothly. Do not anticipate the first beat. (The audio track has been programmed to allow for human reaction time, which is approximately one-fifth of a second.) As soon as you hear it (1), start the clubhead back.

React to the second tone (2) by setting the wrists (2A) and returning the club to the ball at impact. Your club **should** still be moving backward when you hear the second beat.

2. Top of backswing

2A. Setting the wrists

When you have timed your impact with the third beat (3) and are in your finish, hold that finish position (4) in a **freeze frame** until you hear the first beat of the next series.

Concentrate on timing your swing to the beats, but pause from time to time to review your swing fundamentals. Make certain that you are still making a mechanically sound L-drill swing. The club shaft should be pointing back down the target line at (2), top of backswing. The three dimensions of (4), the finish, should still conform to the accompanying photographs.

When you have timed your impact with the third beat and are in your finish, remember to **freeze that finish position** until you hear the first beat of the new series.

3. Impact

4. Finish position

I have a friend, Dennis Kindle, who is a black belt in Okinawan Kenpo, a martial art dating back to pre-feudal Japan. To reach black belt, he took three two-hour classes per week for 14 years. He then added a fourth two-hour class.

"My sensei was very strict on the basics," says Dennis. "These basic forms—stances, punches, blocks, and kicks—are called Kata, and they must be practiced regularly before going on to the more advanced moves. Beginning students frequently get bored going over the basics again and again, but they must practice these moves to train their bodies to respond in the most effective way, without thinking."

According to Dennis, the black belts usually stay after the regular Saturday morning class for another two hours of black-belt training. Beginning students are not allowed to watch these sessions. One Saturday, however, his sensei told the beginner class that they could stay and observe.

"Some of the beginner students were very excited, thinking they were going to see some really neat advanced moves. However, their elation quickly faded. The black belt workout started with the same Kata they were so bored with. Of course, these basic Kata were being done on a much higher level—sharper, stronger, smoother, more fluid, the end of each move serving as the beginning of the next. The beginners didn't understand that if your basics are poor, anything you attempt using that basic skill will be done poorly. On the other hand, when you sharpen a basic skill, anything and everything you do with that skill improves automatically."

Dennis's summation: "When your basics are good and strong, anything you do looks easy and effortless."

I teach tempo, not Kenpo, but I have a similar message for my golf students: "When you faithfully practice the fundamental movements of the Tour Tempo Workout, your swing will start to look easy and effortless—just like the tour pros."

Anyone who has had a golf lesson knows what happens when you try to apply a swing change for the first time. You top the ball. You hit it sideways. You pop it in the air. "You'll get worse before you get better," your chuckling pro explains. Or, "It takes twenty-one days of repetition to master any new motor skill."

Tour Tempo works on a different timetable. Improvement comes in minutes and hours, not days or weeks; the typical pupil hits only one or two bad shots before making solid contact and sending the ball far downrange to a chorus of disbelieving yelps. Tour Tempo confirms Fred Shoemaker's insight that golf learning can be an "all-at-once phenomenon."

Continued improvement and consistency on the course will come from the regular performance of the Tour Tempo Workout.

The 27/9 Tour Tempo Track with the Full Swing

"First Beat" "Second Beat" "Third Beat" "Finish Position"

As in the previous drills, address the ball or impact target and match your swing to the three beats of **27/9 Pre-shot,** the 27/9 track. Make sure that you take the club back smoothly and do not anticipate the beats.

Once the second beat has sounded, start your club swinging back to impact. Since this is a full swing, the club will have a (2) top of backswing somewhere in the neighborhood of the two pictures shown in the previous *24/8 Tour Tempo Track with the L Drill* (2 and 2A). As the club moves from backswing to forward swing, there will be a slight "lag." You should let the (2) top of backswing position occur naturally with the beats, with no conscious effort to control that position.

As in the drills, your goal is to time the sound of impact to the sound of the third beat.

When you have timed your impact with the third beat and are in your follow-through, hold your finish position (4) in a **freeze frame** until you hear the first beat of the new series.

8

Transferring Your New Skills to the Course

"I'll hit it fine on the range," a golfer complained recently in *Golf Digest,* "but the minute I go to the course, it's gone."

The golfer, believe it or not, was Arnold Palmer.

We've all been in Arnie's shoes. No, we haven't won major championships or holed big-money putts in Skins Games, but we've all had that "taking it to the course" problem. You can hit it great on the range and then hook or slice off the first tee. Conversely, you can hit it poorly on the range and then play a great round. What's with that?

One of the problems with "taking it to the course" is that before Tour Tempo, golfers had to use mechanical means to access their A-games. They shifted their weight, lifted their chins, turned their hips, held their spine angles—the whole twenty-point checklist. This type of logical thinking engages the left brain and produces beta and alpha brain waves. When these waves predominate, the brain processes information through your conscious, verbal, logical, and analytical mind. You figure things out step-by-step, one thing following another in logical order.

Golf, unfortunately, is not a left-brain game. To play in "the zone"—that blissful state in which time slows down and you become totally absorbed in what you are doing—you need to access the *right* hemisphere of your brain. When you process information through the right hemisphere, you produce "theta" waves. That leads to the "Ah-ha!" response—the moment when everything seems to fall into place without logical thinking. When a pro says, "Something just clicked on the range this morning, and I started hitting the ball real well," he is describing the shift from left-brain to right-brain activity.

This is the Holy Grail of golf.

The beauty of Tour Tempo is that it trains you for this sort of natural, reflexive ball-striking. But since you're reading this in a book—an alpha-wave activity—here are five logical, step-by-step, left-brain tips to help you "take it to the course."

1. Establish a Pre-shot Routine

Routines that we follow over and over are easier to perform. If you already have a pre-shot routine that works for you, by all means, use it. If not, we recommend the kind of conditioned-response routine used by many great golfers from Bobby Jones to Tiger Woods.

Your pre-shot routine should include a "trigger motion"—a partial swing that rehearses the full swing and confirms the *feel* of the shot. (Woods hovers his clubhead above the ball and rehearses the takeaway. Mike Weir takes the club halfway back and checks its position before placing the clubhead back behind the ball.) A great "trigger motion" is the "Brush the Grass" drill shown on the CD. The entire pre-shot routine is fully explained on the Tour Tempo CD.

What you are doing with your pre-shot routine is "conditioning a response." Conditioned responses are powerful and difficult to break. Once you've established a pre-shot routine, you won't need to worry about how to "start" your golf swing; it will start automatically with the pre-shot. (Billy Casper's pre-shot routine began when he took the club out of the bag. If something disrupted his preparation, he would put the club back in the bag and start over.) With a good pre-shot routine, you will never freeze over the ball, thinking about that twenty-point checklist.

> Never expect a new swing thought to last more than one day.
>
> —Johnny Miller

The pre-shot routine is so important that you should also do it before every practice shot you hit on the range. Perform your routine while listening to three cycles of the tempo tones. Then start your swing, as usual, on the first beat. (I start my backswing by putting my clubhead down behind the ball. That is the first in a sequence of moves cued by the three cycles of Tour Tempo tones.)

The pre-shot routine is best learned by viewing the CD.

Try this quick test. Without looking at a keyboard or your hands, say what finger hits the "P" key and which types the "C" key.

My bet is, you can't do it. But once you're over the keyboard and can see where the keys are in relation to your hands, it's a snap.

That's what we're trying to accomplish with the pre-shot routine. We want to convert a slow, halting, left-brain action into a rapid, reflexive, right-brain action.

---

2. Develop Your Awareness and Feel

As you practice the Y and L drills to the Tour Tempo tones, focus on the *sensations* that accompany your movements. For example, when I do the Y drill it sometimes feels as though all I'm doing is straightening out my wrists to move from the top of the backswing to the finish of the drill. On the days this happens, I feel like I'm swinging like Julius Boros.

Other days, it will be something else. A golfer's "feel" differs from day to day, so you may want to focus on the clubhead, the shaft, the grip, the finish—whatever is the feel or image you want to cultivate that day.

Do not, however, concentrate on the twenty-point checklist. If you start focusing on swing mechanics, the quality of your shot-making will quickly decline. Just go with the flow.

3. Turn Down Your Left-Brain Dimmer Switch

If you are like the vast majority of our students, tempo training will have an immediate and positive effect. Your swing will look smoother, more athletic, more powerful. Your swing will be "prettier." You will hit your range balls farther.

The real purpose of Tour Tempo, however, is *game improvement.* Better tempo produces straighter and longer shots. Straighter and longer shots produce lower scores. Lower scores produce more enjoyment.

Here's the good news: the 3-to-1 Tour Tempo ratio is not something that leaves your swing the minute you take off the headphones. Once you have programmed it into your subconscious mind, you can take it onto any golf course and play relaxed, confident golf, unburdened by those twenty-point checklists and inhibiting "don'ts." (*Don't* move your head on the takeaway! *Don't* let your left heel come off the ground! *Don't* come over the top! . . .)

This is not an outrageous claim. After all, an accomplished typist doesn't have to look to see which finger hits which key. He probably doesn't even *know* which finger hits which key—that information was turned over to his subconscious years ago when he learned to type. It's the same with Tour Tempo and the golf swing. You practice the correct mechanics in your living room or on the range, keying them into your subconscious at the correct tempo. Before long, you have transformed your golf swing into a "reflex action." You will find this reflex swing to be suitable for any shot on the golf course, including pitching and chipping.

If you simply can't imagine playing golf without a list of don'ts, here's a short list of negatives you *can* take to the course:

- **Do not** attempt to reach any particular position at the top of the backswing. *With Tour Tempo you don't have to think about this.*
- **Do not** try to deliberately cock your wrists or even consciously feel the cocking of the wrists. *With Tour Tempo you don't have to think about this.*
- **Do not** try to start your downswing with a deliberate forward thrust of the right knee. *With Tour Tempo the downswing starts automatically.*

In short, you should not try to consciously control any of the swing mechanics you have saved to your internal hard drive. All you have to do to hit a good shot is swing the club away from the ball and back through the ball at the practiced tempo. You may be aware of slight subconscious corrections that your hands and arms are making in order to strike the ball squarely. Only observe these corrections; do not try to make them consciously.

This letting go is necessary in order to allow the swing you have internalized through tempo training to work to its fullest potential.

4. Use Our Tour Tempo Tools to Help Access "the Zone"

The Tour Tempo tones, by keeping you absorbed in the task of listening and responding, will automatically get you closer to the zone. For a further boost, we have recorded some special music on another Tour Tempo CD that you can play on the way to the course—or while you're warming up, or while actually playing—to get and keep the tones in your subconscious mind. (We've all had the experience of listening to a song and then not being able to get it out of our mind. That's what we want to do with these scientifically mastered tracks.) The CD includes songs from country-western, pop, and other genres.

There are also Tour Tempo relaxation tapes that do the same thing for your subconscious. These are best used before a round or at home in a quiet setting. They, too, are specially mastered to help ingrain the correct tempo.

Both of these CDs can be ordered through our website, www.TourTempo.com.

5. Keep Up with the Latest Information from Our Website

Go to TourTempo.com and sign up for our free e-zine newsletter. It will keep you up-to-date on what's happening with Tour Tempo and pass along any new research findings that can help your golf game.

9

Frequently Asked Questions

How fast will I see results?

Since you are working on the most important aspect of the golf swing, you should see results immediately. Most of our students show an instant jump in clubhead speed of from 5 to 20 miles per hour with a 5-iron. That translates to a yardage gain of up to 40 yards. Accuracy generally improves just as quickly, because proper tempo discourages casting or flipping the clubhead through the impact position.

These results fly in the face of conventional wisdom, which says that it takes twenty-one days of repetitive practice to master any motor skill. The difference with Tour Tempo is this: You aren't learning a new motor skill, you are merely performing it with the most advantageous timing.

As the old saying goes, "You can't cross a chasm in small steps." Sometimes you have to make a big jump.

Which is more important, the 3-to-1 ratio or the overall elapsed time of my swing?

The 3-to-1 ratio. If you want to play like a pro, both of them are important. But the accomplished amateur will gain more by mastering the ratio than by trying to swing as fast as Ben Hogan.

What do I do if my swing is already faster than the 27/9 Tour Tempo track?

Is your name Ed Furgol? The 1954 U.S. Open champion is the only tour player I have timed who could beat all three of the Tour Tempo audio tracks to the finish line. Furgol's swing, an 18/6, was practically a lightning strike. He took less than eight-tenths of a second from takeaway to impact.

So yes, your swing could be faster than 27/9 Pre-shot, our primary training track. If you find that the 27/9 tones are slower than your current swing, by all means, move up to the 24/8 or 21/7 Tour Tempo tracks.

Can I swing slower than 27/9 if I maintain the 3-to-1 ratio?

I've relaxed my view on this. I recently had my own swing timed on the course, and I clocked a 260-yard drive down the middle with a 33/11 swing. I was not *trying* to swing that slowly—I'd like to be at 27/9, and I train with 21/7—but I'm an old guy and not in the best shape. Furthermore, I'm like most amateurs; when I get on the golf course, my swing tends to get a little longer than I would like. I still hit the ball fine as long as I maintain the 3-to-1 ratio.

John Novosel, Jr. has long argued that some golfers should get into Tour Tempo the way a bather slips into a hot tub—gradually, getting used to the heat in stages. Others have pointed out to me that a golfer making a swing change has to slow his swing down temporarily to master the new move. For these golfers, practicing to slowed-down Tour Tempo tracks might be beneficial. Consequently, I have added "hot tub" audio tracks of 30/10 and 33/11 to the Tour Tempo CD.

I still don't teach anything slower than 27/9 because anything slower is not up to tour standards, and because most amateurs need to speed up to get some athleticism into their swings. A ratio of 36/12, in my view, is way too slow. What good is perfect timing if you can't hit the ball out of your shadow?

If I get comfortable with 27/9, should I speed up to 24/8?

If you are happy with your game at 27/9, I see no reason to change.

On the other hand, you could follow the example of Tiger Woods. Tiger had perfect 27/9 timing in 1997, when he won his first Masters and player-of-the-year honors, but he had a few swing flaws. Working on those swing defects in '98, Tiger won only one tournament and had his worst year as a pro. In 1999, when his swing changes finally clicked, he won the PGA Championship and nine other tournaments. He had perfect timing again—only now he was a 24/8.

Here's the amazing part. Tiger didn't shorten his elapsed time by curtailing his swing, as many pros do. He had a relatively short backswing to begin with—about three-quarters with his driver—and after a year's work with swing coach Butch Harmon he was swinging all the way to the top. In other words, the old Tiger took 27 frames to take the clubhead back about 9 feet. Now he needs only 24 frames to take the clubhead back 12 feet.

Still following? If we break his swing down into "feet per frame (fpf)" and compare his new backswing (12 feet in 24 frames = .5 fpf) to his old backswing (9 feet in 27 frames = .3 fpf), we reach a startling conclusion: *Tiger's new backswing is 66 percent faster.*

So much for "nobody ever swung a golf club too slowly."

I would add that in 1998, when Woods struggled, he was focusing on swing mechanics. That probably retarded his tempo. By the middle of

’98, as he got comfortable with the swing changes, he played again with little or no conscious awareness of technique. The result: a perfect 24/8 swing and a roomful of trophies.

So, I *should* try for 24/8 . . . or even 21/7?

Not if you have to dramatically rush your downswing to get there.

To see if you’re a candidate for a faster tempo, make a digital video of your swing. Download the video into an editing program and check the frame count for a representative sample of swings. If some of your forward swings clock at 8 frames, that’s a good sign that you should be aiming for the 24/8 standard. If you average 9 or 10 frames, stick with 27/9.

How can thirty-three thousandths of a second be so important?

Because that’s about how long the clubface is on the ball during an entire round.

Spalding Sporting Goods ran a golf lab in the 1930s. Using high-speed photography, the company’s engineers determined that a ball was in contact with the clubface for only .0004 seconds on a typical shot. Assuming that you take 80 strokes over eighteen holes, the ball is on the clubface for only .032 seconds per round.

The most important reason, however, is that if it’s the frame before impact, your clubhead can travel approximately 3 feet during that thirty-three thousandths of a second.

This is shown in the accompanying illustrations. On the left is the club one frame away and 3 feet away from impact. On the right the club is shown at impact.

The clubhead can travel the final three feet to impact in just thirty-three thousandths of a second.

Do I have to do the Y and L drills for Tour Tempo to work?

If you already have decent swing mechanics, no. But if your swing is fundamentally flawed, it is important that you master the Y and L drills. They provide the framework of the modern golf swing. Do them to the best of your ability and you will improve.

Do I have to remember a lot of stuff when I take Tour Tempo out on the golf course?

No. Tour Tempo makes the golf swing a reflex or instinctive action. A stimulus comes in, and without conscious thought your body answers with an outward response.

That's what makes Tour Tempo very different from traditional instruction. The old paradigm asks you to "connect the dots" while swinging. (I shift my weight . . . now I cock my wrists . . . now I point my elbow outward . . . ad nauseam.) With a reflex action you don't have to *think*. You don't have to remember a *twenty-point checklist*. You don't get hung up on biomechanics.

Will a slight increase in clubhead speed significantly affect how far I hit the ball?

Absolutely. According to *The Search for the Perfect Swing,* the definitive study on the application of science to the golf swing, clubhead speed at impact is the main factor in determining distance. It's physics. You want to carry the ball 254 yards through the air with your driver? Then you must have a clubhead speed of 110 miles per hour at impact (see accompanying chart). If you're using a legal club, it makes no difference what material it's made of, how it's constructed, or what the length of the shaft is. If your clubhead is not going 110 miles per hour at impact, you are not going to carry the ball 254 yards.

But look at what you gain with a "slight" improvement in clubhead speed. An 80-miles-per-hour 5-iron flies 18 yards farther than a 70-miles-per-hour 5-iron. A 100-miles-per-hour drive flies 22 yards farther than a 90-miles-per-hour drive.

Yes, other factors do affect distance—launch angle and spin rate, to name two—but clubhead speed is still the principal power ingredient.

How do I know I am increasing my clubhead speed?

Since 1992 we have measured the clubhead speeds of all our students with the SwingMate®, a portable radar device made by Beltronics. The yardage you actually hit a ball is influenced by wind, terrain, ball composition, and spin, but clubhead speed provides a reliable benchmark for golfers of all abilities. (The touring pros, it goes without saying, measure their clubhead speeds on a regular basis.) We have also found the SwingMate® to be helpful in short-game practice. By varying your clubhead speed while performing the L drill, you can master distance control on pitch shots.

We do not recommend, however, that you beat balls on the range with a speed gun, like some carnival dandy trying to ring the bell. Any effort to muscle up or "race" the clubhead through the ball will destroy your tempo and actually slow down your swing.

DISTANCE MATRIX

MPH TO PRODUCE YARDS IN BALL FLIGHT (CARRY)

5-IRON

50 MPH = 93 YDS
70 MPH = 130 YDS
71 MPH = 132 YDS
72 MPH = 134 YDS
73 MPH = 136 YDS
74 MPH = 138 YDS
75 MPH = 140 YDS
76 MPH = 142 YDS
77 MPH = 144 YDS
78 MPH = 146 YDS
79 MPH = 148 YDS
80 MPH = 150 YDS
81 MPH = 152 YDS
82 MPH = 154 YDS
83 MPH = 156 YDS
84 MPH = 158 YDS
85 MPH = 159 YDS
86 MPH = 161 YDS
87 MPH = 163 YDS
88 MPH = 165 YDS
89 MPH = 167 YDS
90 MPH = 169 YDS
91 MPH = 170 YDS
92 MPH = 172 YDS
93 MPH = 174 YDS
94 MPH = 176 YDS
95 MPH = 178 YDS
96 MPH = 180 YDS
97 MPH = 184 YDS
98 MPH = 186 YDS
100 MPH = 188 YDS

DISTANCE MATRIX

MPH TO PRODUCE YARDS IN BALL FLIGHT (CARRY)

DRIVER

80 MPH = 184.9 YDS
81 MPH = 187.2 YDS
82 MPH = 189.5 YDS
83 MPH = 191.8 YDS
84 MPH = 194.1 YDS
85 MPH = 196.4 YDS
86 MPH = 198.7 YDS
87 MPH = 201.0 YDS
88 MPH = 203.3 YDS
89 MPH = 205.6 YDS
90 MPH = 207.9 YDS
91 MPH = 210.2 YDS
92 MPH = 212.5 YDS
93 MPH = 214.8 YDS
94 MPH = 217.1 YDS
95 MPH = 219.4 YDS
96 MPH = 221.7 YDS
97 MPH = 224.0 YDS
98 MPH = 226.3 YDS
100 MPH = 231.0 YDS
101 MPH = 233.2 YDS
102 MPH = 235.5 YDS
103 MPH = 237.8 YDS
104 MPH = 240.1 YDS
105 MPH = 242.4 YDS
106 MPH = 244.7 YDS
107 MPH = 247 YDS
108 MPH = 249.5 YDS
109 MPH = 252 YDS
110 MPH – 254 YDS
120 MPH = 277 YDS
130 MPH = 300 YDS

What about my short game? Does Tour Tempo apply to chip shots and short pitches?

Yes, up to a point. Most tour players seem to swing at or near the 3-to-1 ratio when they are hitting from greenside bunkers or pitching to greens from 40 or more yards. It's a different story when they are chipping or hitting finesse shots from greenside rough. (Tiger Woods's chipping tempo is 15/7, or about 2-to-1.) My rule of thumb is: Anytime your backswing takes the club to a point where it is parallel or past parallel to the ground, Tour Tempo applies. If your shot doesn't require that long a backswing, you don't need a 3-to-1 swing.

Personally, I like to practice chipping and putting to the 21/7 audio track. Good timing and a smooth stroke make a difference, even when the hole is only a few feet away.

Does every touring pro exhibit the 3-to-1 ratio on every swing?

Ah, if only life were that simple. Golfers aren't robots, and we're talking about taking measurements in thousandths of a second. What we are saying is that a majority of world-class players, when they are playing their best, adhere to this tempo constant. Furthermore, the very best of the best—which, at this writing, would be Tiger Woods and Annika Sorenstam—achieve the 3-to-1 ratio on almost every swing.

Do I have to have a 3-to-1 tempo to play decent golf?

Tough question. Nancy Lopez, the LPGA Hall of Famer, now takes a painful-to-watch 50 frames to complete her backswing and 10 more frames to get back to impact. When she was winning tournaments in the 1970s, however, her numbers were 30/10—the same as today's wunderkind, Michelle Wie. Imagine what Nancy's record would have been had she kept her 3-to-1 tempo through the years.

So, yes, you can play with a tempo ratio different from Tour Tempo's. But unless you play and practice golf seven days a week, we

Celebrity Golfers

Television doesn't devote much air time to the swings of recreational golfers, but I sometimes hit the RECORD button when the cameras capture celebrities at play. Some of these celebrity swings come surprisingly close to the Tour Tempo ratio. But remember, some of these tempo ratios were taken from edited-for-television events, and only the best shots were shown. (Typically, amateurs approximate the desired 3-to-1 ratio several times per round, producing the great shots that keep them interested in golf.)

In other words, these tempo numbers may not represent the celebrities' usual games. On the other hand, some of the celebs are single-digit handicappers and the swings analyzed might actually represent their Tempo IQ.

Bob Hope, 19/6. Hope was good enough to qualify for the 1951 British Amateur and at one time carried a 4 handicap.
Pete Sampras, 22/8
Mark McGuire, 22/7
Rush Limbaugh, 23/9 (maybe too much weight on his right side?), 18 handicap
Jeremy Roenik, 19/9
Rodney Dangerfield (Al Czervic in the movie *Caddyshack*), 14/6
Michael O'Keefe (Danny Noonan in *Caddyshack*), 28/9—Attaboy, Nooner!
Martin Sheen, 18/7, 17 handicap
Alice Cooper, 26/9, 7 handicap
Samuel L. Jackson, 25/8, 9 handicap
James Woods, 22/7, 16 handicap
Michael Douglas, 23/7, 20 handicap
Catherine Zeta-Jones, 26/10
Thomas Gibson, 25/7, 7 handicap
Don Cheadle, 26/10, 19 handicap
Haley Joel Osment, 27/10
Jim McClean (noted golf instructor and author), 21/7

don't think your swing will be as consistent as the Tour Tempo swing. And we're certain it will not hold up as well under pressure.

Can I play a round of golf while listening to the Tour Tempo tones and then submit the score for handicap purposes?

Under current USGA rules, you would be violating Rule 14-3. (". . . The player shall not use any artificial device or unusual equipment . . . which might assist him in making a stroke or in his play.") On the other hand, there is no penalty for listening while warming up on the range or walking to the first tee. The rules may have to be modified if players start turning up at Member/Guests with cords dangling from their ears and faraway looks in their eyes. I personally love to listen to the various Tour Tempo songs in between shots when I'm playing a practice round or "emergency nine."

How often should I practice to the Tour Tempo tracks?

The more often you practice with the Tour Tempo Workout, the better your on-course game will become. If you neglect the Workout, however, you may suffer the fate of Ben Hogan, who, paraphrasing the classical pianist Paderewski, said, "If I miss a day of practice, I notice it. If I miss two days of practice, my fans notice it." I personally try to use the Tour Tempo Workout as a warm-up before every round of golf.

So use it on the range. Use it in practice rounds. If you have a few minutes, go out in your backyard and simply brush the grass with a club while listening to the audio tracks.

There is just one caveat. The minute you lose focus, stop the CD. You have to concentrate on the beats in order to program your inner clock.

Do I risk injury by swinging at a faster tempo?

I don't see how. A fast, smooth tempo is much kinder to the body than the jerky, lurching motion of the high handicapper. Typically the player who is trying to swing "low and slow" takes the club back as if it weighs 20 pounds. He then races down from the top with a forward slide and a back-wrenching spin. Ouch!

The Tour Tempo swing is quick, but it promotes better balance. That's good for the body. Most golf injuries are sustained when the spine and joints are stressed by a wobbly, off-balance follow-through. Of course, if you have a preexisting medical condition you should consult a doctor before training with Tour Tempo or any other sports or exercise program.

Can an absolute beginner use the Tour Tempo system?

Yes. Since tempo is one of the fundamentals of golf, it can only help the beginner to learn the game with the correct timing. However, the novice golfer still has to learn the other fundamentals of the game—grip, stance, etc. That's why we recommend the Y and L drills. (We haven't included information about grip, stance, or alignment in this book, because there is abundant existing instruction on this. For our take on those subjects, you can visit our website.)

I'm a senior golfer. Am I too old and slow for Tour Tempo?

Not at all. As long as you have some flexibility and solid leg support, you will benefit from proper tempo. In fact, Tour Tempo should allow you to recover some of the yardage that Old Man Time has taken away. Clubhead speed is determined by technique and tempo, not raw strength.

I can use myself as an example. Many decades ago, when I played football at Kansas State University, I was strong enough to press my wife over my head—and that's very hard to do with live weight. The last couple of years, however, I have suffered from Lyme disease and kidney stones, and I have lost about half the muscle mass in my arms. Even so, I now hit the golf ball farther than at any other time in my life. It's all about technique and timing.

Granted, you may not be able to take as full a backswing as you did when you were younger. Tom Watson's swing is shorter than it used to be. His tempo, however, remains a brisk 24/7, and he is probably a more consistent ball-striker today than he was in his youth.

What's the biggest misconception about Tour Tempo training that students have to overcome?

The biggest problem students have with the training regimen is that they confuse the instructions for the second tone with the instructions for the third tone. They try to make their top of backswing line up with the second tone.

And that's OK with the Swing-Set drill, when you're learning how the first two Tour Tempo beats work to coordinate the speed and the length of your backswing to fit the Y and L drills; or when you are experimenting with different top of backswing positions. (To achieve a John Daly-length backswing, for example, you would have to speed up your backswing.)

But that's not how it works when you go to the three beats. While the third tone should line up with or coincide with the sound and feel of impact, the second tone is the golfer's signal to set the wrists and return to impact. The first and second tones are *reflexive* only. You react to a stimulus. The club should still be moving when you hear the second tone.

Once again, when using the three beats:

1. The first and second tones signal a response to a stimulus.
2. The third tone is the only tone that lines up with something—impact.

So only react reflexively to the first and second tones. When you drill in this manner, the three Tour Tempo tones will set up the correct sequencing of the body and make your swing an athletic, graceful movement.

Analysis

PART THREE

10

Case Studies

CASE STUDY 32-02

Name: Bruce Provo

Occupation: Businessman **Age:** 52

Handicap: 9

Average Carry with Driver: 208 yards

Average Carry with 5-iron: 148 yards

Self-Evaluation: "Overthinking is my biggest problem. I also have trouble finishing my swings. I'm a great steerer. I go to right *here* . . ." (Demonstrating a follow-through, Bruce freezes the clubhead and his hands a little past waist height.) "And that's as far as I get. And obviously I don't hit the ball as far as I think I should."

Trainer: John Novosel

Training Site: Hallbrook Country Club, Leawood, Kansas

Test Swings (3 representative swings)

	Clubhead Speed at Impact			Frames Ratio			Total Elapsed Time in Seconds		
	Swing 1	Swing 2	Swing 3	Swing 1	Swing 2	Swing 3	Swing 1	Swing 2	Swing 3
5-iron	79 MPH	74MPH	77 MPH	44/11	45/11	46/11	1.83	1.87	1.90
Driver	90 MPH	84 MPH	91 MPH	46/10	45/11	44/10	1.87	1.87	1.80

Diagnosis: Bruce's mechanics and ball flight are quite good. He hits a consistent draw and makes solid contact on most of his swings. On the other hand, his clubhead speeds are quite slow for a player of his ability. He seems to be overcontrolling the club through impact and not really compressing the ball. His tempo, measured on the computer, is 44/11. That's pretty pokey, a 4-to-1 ratio. A swing that slow tends to break down under pressure.

Training Report: I started Bruce with the 27/9 tempo track, a 5-iron, and no ball. To lessen the shock to his system, I had Bruce "preset" the club in his backswing (see accompanying photo) with the shaft parallel to the ground. I then asked him to start his swing from that position when he heard the first beep. Even so, Bruce was amazed at the pace of the tones. "I just feel like I'm moving so *fast,*" he said, trying to brush the grass in time to the third beat. However, the minute I put some balls down for Bruce, he began hitting 5-irons that flew high over the flag he was aiming at. "I've never hit a 5-iron like that," he said. "I've never hit the ball so solid."

With the headphones on, Bruce couldn't hear that crisp sound of solid compression. But he only had to glance at the digital SwingMate® on the ground to see that his clubhead speed had jumped into the upper 80s and low 90s. His wife, Betsy, amazed by the shots he was hitting, laughed out loud. She said, "Are you loving yourself?"

Once he was used to the faster tempo, I had Bruce start his backswing from his normal address position. He immediately recorded clubhead speeds of 95 and 99 miles per hour and drilled several shots completely over the target green, 185 yards away. "Twenty minutes ago, I was kind of tired," Bruce said, eagerly raking another ball into position. "I'm not so tired now!"

Bruce Provo, Before & After 30-Minute Tempo Training Session

	Average Clubhead Speed at Impact		Estimated Carry		Frames Ratio		Total Elapsed Time in Seconds	
	Before	After	Before	After	Before	After	Before	After
5-iron	77 MPH	95MPH	144	178	45/11	31/10	1.83	1.35
Driver	90 MPH	107 MPH	208	247	46/11	31/10	1.88	1.35

Follow-Up: Two days after his training session, I played nine holes with Bruce at Hallbrook Country Club. On the seventh hole, a long par-4, Bruce drove the ball 265 yards (lasered by John Novosel, Jr.). On the fourth hole, a long par-5, Bruce got home in two with a 228-yard 4-wood to a small green guarded in front by a stream. "Your swing doesn't look faster," Betsy told Bruce, "but the ball is definitely going farther."

On average, Bruce gained almost 40 yards with his driver and about 25 yards with his 5-iron. In the weeks that followed, he reported that his new swing held up better under pressure, too. "I don't get lost at the top of the backswing the way I used to. And I don't get confused by a bunch of swing thoughts. I don't have *time* to think."

CASE STUDY 61-02

Name: John Ross

Occupation: Business owner **Age:** 50

Handicap: 17

Average Carry with Driver: 240 yards

Average Carry with 5-iron: 170 yards

Self-Evaluation: "Every time I think I've cured my slice, I seem to revert to my old ways. I've read instruction books and the tips in the golf magazines, but how do you hit the ball when you've got a million things to think of?"

Trainer: John Novosel, Jr.

Training Site: Twin Oaks Driving Range, Lawrence, Kansas

Test Swings (3 representative swings)

	Clubhead Speed at Impact			Frames Ratio			Total Elapsed Time in Seconds		
	Swing 1	Swing 2	Swing 3	Swing 1	Swing 2	Swing 3	Swing 1	Swing 2	Swing 3
5-iron	94 MPH	76 MPH (fat shot)	94 MPH	25/11	25/10	27/10	1.2	1.17	1.23
Driver	103 MPH	105 MPH	102 MPH	27/11	28/10	27/11	1.27	1.27	1.27

Diagnosis: When John first came to me, he wanted to get rid of his slice. We worked on his mechanics some, and he's gone from shooting in the low 50s for nine holes to shooting in the low 40s. But he still tends to cast and lunge. That's why he leaves the clubface open at impact, and it's why his most solidly struck shots are extreme pushes and push-fades. Despite pretty good clubhead speed, John says he has never hit his 7-iron more than 150 yards. In my opinion, his game won't improve until he learns how to square up the clubface at impact.

Training Report: I started John with the preset drill and the 24/8 Tour Tempo audio track. I had him brush the grass with the 5-iron for a few swings, and then I let him hit some balls with the preset drill. Interestingly, his clubhead speed on his first two swings *dropped* about 6 miles per hour, possibly because of tension. Both shots, however, were almost dead straight. He then nuked one, a 96-miles-per-hour pull-hook that I lasered at 170 yards. "That felt *really* good," John said. "I don't think I've ever hit a 5-iron that solidly." He then hit a series of high draws with clubhead speeds in the high 80s.

The best was still to come. When I told John to quit the preset drill and start his backswing from the normal position, he got his clubhead speed up to the low 90s. Every single shot had the desired right-to-left flight, including his "misses," which were now pull-hooks. When I saw that John was getting a little rigid while anticipating the takeaway beep, I told him, "Don't be standing there motionless. I want to see a little movement." John promptly crushed a 96-miles-per-hour 5-iron right over his target flag, a shot that I lasered at 175 yards.

"Is the tape running?" he asked. "That was orgasmic!"

John Ross, Before & After 30-Minute Tempo Training Session

	Average Clubhead Speed at Impact		Estimated Carry		Frames Ratio		Total Elapsed Time in Seconds	
	Before	After	Before	After	Before	After	Before	After
5-iron	88 MPH	92 MPH	165	172	26/10	24/9	1.2	1.1
Driver	103 MPH	---	237.8	---	27/11	---	1.27	---

Follow-Up: "The tones are amazing," John said at the end of his tempo lesson. "You guys didn't tell me what to do, you didn't give me a list of things to think about. You just put the headphones on me and said 'go.' After that, it was just listen and react. It was like I was getting a golf lesson from Pavlov." When we timed John's "after" swings on the computer, we found that his tempo ratio had improved to 24/9. And while his casting action did not entirely disappear, as often happens with tempo training, he seemed to time his cast better, taming that slice. A year later, on August 23, 2003, John shot 33-38-71 at Eagle Bend Golf Club in Lawrence, Kansas, his best score ever.

CASE STUDY 107-02

Name: Bob Walsh

Occupation: Retired telecom executive **Age:** 57

Handicap: 22

Average Carry with Driver: 220 yards

Average Carry with 5-iron: 165 yards

Self-Evaluation: "I've been playing golf about thirteen years, but I never improve. I tried to rebuild my swing with a pro a few years ago, but it didn't work. I was thinking about too much—a new ball placement, stretching my arms out, elbows in. My handicap actually went up. When I got rid of all those swing thoughts, I felt more relaxed and played a little better. . . . I hit my irons okay—not far, but I can put them where I want. But I'm not consistent off the tee box. I resort to the 3-wood most of the time because at least I can keep the 3-wood in play. . . . I think my tempo goes from real slow to real fast, depending on who I'm playing with. As the round goes on, I lose concentration and start to swing faster."

Trainer: John Novosel

Training Site: Iron Horse Golf Club, Leawood, Kansas

Test Swings (3 representative swings)

	Clubhead Speed at Impact			Frames Ratio			Total Elapsed Time in Seconds		
	Swing 1	Swing 2	Swing 3	Swing 1	Swing 2	Swing 3	Swing 1	Swing 2	Swing 3
5-iron	87 MPH	96 MPH	81 MPH	41/10	39/9	41/11	1.70	1.60	1.73
Driver	---	---	---	---	---	---	---	---	---

Diagnosis: It's hard to believe that Bob is a 20-handicapper. His posture and setup are excellent, and his smooth backswing is to die for. He makes an excellent shoulder turn, has good arm extension, and his hand action at the top is as firm as a pro's. He doesn't cast the club coming down, either. Bob's only obvious flaw is that he doesn't quite move his weight onto his left side in an aggressive, athletic manner. That's because his tempo is glacial. His swing looks slow to the naked eye, and his test swings confirm it: He's 44/11, a tempo ratio of 4-to-1. With such a slow, mistimed swing, Bob produces wildly inconsistent clubhead speeds and finds it almost impossible to square the clubface at impact.

Training Report: I started Bob with a 5-iron and the 27/9 Tour Tempo track. To prevent "speed shock," I had him start his backswing from the waist-high, preset position. He hit a few clunkers, but quickly got the feel of the faster tempo. When I let him start his swing from the normal position, he spanked some great-looking shots with clubhead speeds in the low to mid-90s. The biggest improvements were in launch direction (straighter) and trajectory (lower). His clubhead speed with the 5-iron remained inconsistent, ranging from 88 to 106 miles per hour, but it was consistently faster than before. . . . When Bob switched to the driver, he got a little "ball-bound" and hit some erratic shots with no improvement in clubhead speed. So I had him hit some more irons. He immediately regained his feel with the 5-iron. After a while he picked up a wedge and hit some excellent shots with clubhead speeds in the 78–80 miles-per-hour range. "The ball is flying really nice," he said. "Higher than before and farther than before, even with the short irons. I never thought I could swing the club that fast and keep it under control."

Bob Walsh, Before & After 30-Minute Tempo Training Session

	Average Clubhead Speed at Impact		Estimated Carry		Frames Ratio		Total Elapsed Time in Seconds	
	Before	After	Before	After	Before	After	Before	After
5-iron	88 MPH	105 MPH	165	198	40/10	26/8	1.67	1.13
Driver	---	---	---	---	---	---	---	---

Follow-Up: Bob's swing mechanics were so good that he had no difficulty matching the Tour Tempo beats. Swinging at 27/9, he improved his weight shift, which made the ball fly straighter and longer at a better trajectory. To illustrate the improvement, I produced a tape of Bob's before and after swings and put them side-by-side with Al Geiberger's benchmark swing. In the first swing comparison, Bob's swing is so slow that Geiberger is into his follow-through before Bob completes his backswing. In the second comparison, Bob's Tour Tempo swing matches Geiberger's from takeaway to follow-through.

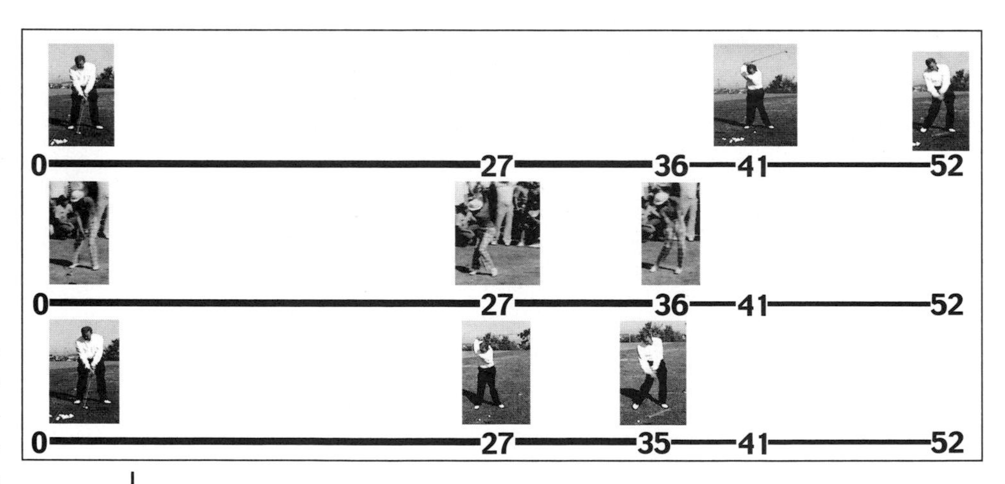

Comparison of Bob's before and after swings versus the Tour Tempo model, Al Geiberger

More important, Bob's scoring also showed improvement. Within weeks he lowered his handicap by six strokes, to sixteen. "I feel more confident playing," he wrote in an e-mail. "Everyone I play with comments on my swing. I feel my backswing is fast, but they all think it is great. Thanks for your help. I can't wait until you share this with other struggling golfers."

CASE STUDY 33-02

Name: Betsy Provo

Occupation: Human resources manager

Handicap: 6

Average Carry with Driver: 198.7 yards

Average Carry with 5-iron: 148 yards

Trainer: John Novosel

Training Site: Hallbrook Country Club, Leawood, Kansas

Test Swings (3 representative swings)

	Clubhead Speed at Impact			Frames Ratio			Total Elapsed Time in Seconds		
	Swing 1	Swing 2	Swing 3	Swing 1	Swing 2	Swing 3	Swing 1	Swing 2	Swing 3
5-iron	81 MPH	77 MPH	78 MPH	33/9	34/9	35/9	1.40	1.43	1.47
Driver	86 MPH	85 MPH	87 MPH	---	---	---	---	---	---

Diagnosis: Betsy, a five-time club champion at Hallbrook Country Club, is an accomplished player with a superb swing and a thorough knowledge of the game. When we timed her swing on the computer, she came in between 33/9 and 35/9. Her backswing is only 6 or 7 frames slower than Jan Stephenson's. Betsy hits the high draw favored by many LPGA players, and her clubhead speed with the 5-iron is 78 miles per hour, which means she can fly the ball as far as her husband on most holes. Tempo training probably won't boost her carry that much, because she's already hitting the ball very solidly. But it should improve her consistency, and she'll be able to correct her tempo whenever it goes off.

Training Report: Betsy already swings almost as fast as the 27/9 model, so I started her out with the 5-iron and the 27/9 audio track and let her address the ball normally. "It feels a little weird," she said, trying to time her impact to the second chirp. Her first two or three tries were not pretty; she hit them fat. After that, she made solid contact, but she pushed several shots well right of her target.

On the upside, Betsy's clubhead speed showed immediate improvement. To my eye, however, Betsy was finding it difficult to adapt her grooved swing to the beats. Most students shorten their swings slightly to chase the faster tempo, but Betsy's swing with the headphones on was every bit as full as the ones we had recorded.

When Betsy switched to her 4-wood, she hit a nice high draw (clubhead speed, 88 miles per hour), and then really ripped one, a rocket that flew past all the target flags and rolled down near the tee line at the opposite end of the range. "I love it!" she said. "I think it's great."

I wasn't so sure. With the headphones on, Betsy's swing seemed less natural, less reflexive than before. When Betsy told me that she would be defending her club championship the next week, I discouraged her from working with the tempo tracks until after the tournament. "We'll resume in a couple of weeks and try to lock your tempo in at 27/9," I told her. "But for now, forget about it."

Betsy Provo, Before & After 30-Minute Tempo Training Session

	Average Clubhead Speed at Impact		Estimated Carry		Frames Ratio		Total Elapsed Time in Seconds	
	Before	After	Before	After	Before	After	Before	After
5-iron	79 MPH	83 MPH	148	156	34/9	31/9	1.43	1.33
Driver	88 MPH	91 MPH	203.3	210.2	---	---	---	---

Follow-Up: Betsy successfully defended her club championship, winning the women's stroke-play event by a stroke. She later decided she was happy with her swing the way it was and didn't change it. I supported her decision, saying, "If it ain't broke, don't fix it." After reviewing her training session, I felt she was trying to make the beats correspond to her swing instead of just reflexively reacting to them. Knowing what we know now, I would have started Betsy the way we now start everybody, with the Swing-Set drill.

Drilling on the first two beats would have helped her get accustomed to the whole process. The good news was that she added a couple of yards with the Tour Tempo training and it obviously didn't affect her swing negatively, as she still successfully defended her club title.

CASE STUDY 44-11

Name: Greg Windholz

Occupation: Hospital department manager **Age:** 36

Handicap: 9.4

Average Carry with Driver: 230 yards

Average Carry with 5-iron: 160 yards

Self-Evaluation: "I went ten years without a driver in my bag. I've hit it off houses. Now I've cut about ten strokes from my handicap, thanks to lessons with John, Jr. and my work with the XLR8R®. But my game is still pretty inconsistent. If I swing too hard, I inevitably pull the shot left. I know in my mind that I'm swinging too hard and need to slow down, but I have no swing thought when it comes to tempo."

Trainer: John Novosel, Jr.

Training Site: Eagle Bend Golf Club, Lawrence, Kansas

Test Swings (3 representative swings)

	Clubhead Speed at Impact			Frames Ratio			Total Elapsed Time in Seconds		
	Swing 1	Swing 2	Swing 3	Swing 1	Swing 2	Swing 3	Swing 1	Swing 2	Swing 3
5-iron	81 MPH (topped)	91 MPH (fat shot)	84 MPH (fat shot)	24/9	24/10	24/10	1.10	1.13	1.13
Driver	101 MPH	97 MPH	101 MPH	24/10	24/9	24/10	1.13	1.10	1.13

Diagnosis: Greg is one of the few people I know who plays better on the course than he does on the range. When I watched him hit a few balls for testing purposes, he hit several laterals into the trees to our right. "It's my driving range shank," he said apologetically. "You've seen it a million times."

Seeing isn't always believing. Greg's test swings looked Tour Tempo fast; the clubhead whistled impressively through the ball. His clubhead speeds, however, aren't up to tour standards, and when I timed his swings on the computer I was surprised to find that his tempo ratio is 25/10 or 25/11. In other words, he has a fast backswing and a slow forward swing. Without even breaking down his mechanics, I know what that means. Greg is casting—throwing the club at the ball and losing his wrist angle well before impact. As a result, he hits as many bad shots as good shots, including a lot of fat shots and those dreaded laterals.

Training Report: In a misguided effort to capitalize on Greg's apparent comfort level with a fast swing (the 27/9 Tour Tempo track felt "slow" to him), we started his training with a 5-iron and the 24/8 tape. The results were not pretty. Greg hit a pull-top, a horrible shank, and several very fat shots. Analyzing those swings on the computer later, it was clear that Greg's casting was so severe that his clubhead couldn't catch up to the third tone at impact, even though he was trying to swing very fast. Fooled by this apparent speed, my dad suggested that Greg try the 21/7 track. That only made things worse. Greg's mechanics deteriorated further, and he hit a string of shots that made him look like a thirty-handicapper, not a nine.

Just when we were about to give up, Greg asked if he could go to his car and get his XLR8R®. "When I get too fast," he said, "I can usually smooth myself out with the XLR8R®." Sure enough, when Greg went off to the side of the range and took some swings at the impact target, his rhythm and balance instantly improved. He began to swing *through* the target into a balanced finish position.

Once he had regained this feel, Greg put the headphones back on and returned to the firing line with his 5-iron. What followed was remarkable. Swinging to the 24/8 track, Greg immediately increased his clubhead speed by about 10 miles per hour. His shots began to fly straight to the target with a nice draw. Switching to his driver, he started out a little shaky—a 107-miles-per-hour push and a 102-miles-per-hour duck-hook—but a few more whacks at the XLR8R® fixed that. Greg concluded his training session with a series of long, straight drives of about 260 to 270 yards. "Feels good with the driver," he said. "But you can see what I mean when I say I'm inconsistent."

Greg's post-XLR8R® swings were still a bit off the beat (he was about 26/9 with the 24/8 tape), but his swing was noticeably shorter, the casting was less pronounced, and his downswing speed improved by one to two frames. I suggested that he continue to practice with the XLR8R® and that he work on his tempo with the 27/9 Tour Tempo track.

Greg Windholz, Before & After 30-Minute Tempo Training Session

	Average Clubhead Speed at Impact		Estimated Carry		Frames Ratio		Total Elapsed Time in Seconds	
	Before	After	Before	After	Before	After	Before	After
5-iron	85 MPH	97 MPH	159	184	24/10	26/9	1.13	1.17
Driver	100 MPH	103 MPH	231	238	24/10	26/9	1.13	1.17

Follow-Up: In the weeks following his rocky tempo lesson, Greg broke 80 three times and shot consistently in the low 80s. "The tempo training helped tremendously," he told me after shooting a 77 at the Alvamar Golf Club in Lawrence. "It has helped me slow down a little on the course, which, in turn, has made me much more accurate. Last summer I had never even entertained the thought of breaking 80; it just wasn't in my game." Greg's new goals are to shoot consistently in the 70s and win his flight in the city tournament.

Postscript Fast-forward to one year after Tour Tempo testing: Greg is now consistently shooting in the 70s.

CASE STUDY 3-03

Name: Josh Weems

Occupation: Student **Age:** 12

Average Carry with Driver: NA

Average Carry with 5-iron: 124 yards

Trainer: John Novosel

Training Site: Robin Nigro Golf Academy, Kansas City, Missouri

Test Swings (3 representative swings)

	Clubhead Speed at Impact			Frames Ratio			Total Elapsed Time in Seconds		
	Swing 1	Swing 2	Swing 3	Swing 1	Swing 2	Swing 3	Swing 1	Swing 2	Swing 3
5-iron	67 MPH	68 MPH	66 MPH	39/11	40/11	30/10	1.67	1.70	1.63
Driver	---	---	---	---	---	---	---	---	---

Diagnosis: Josh has great golf movement for a kid. Good high hands on his backswing. A great follow-through. I'm not crazy about his wrist position at the top; he never gets his wrists cocked. He recovers pretty nicely, but he's manipulating the club instead of swinging it. Mostly though, he needs to work on his timing. His tempo ratio of 39/11 costs him distance and fails to take advantage of his youthful flexibility and athleticism.

Training Report: I started Josh on the 27/9 tape and had him do the Y and L drills with an XLR8R® striking club and impact target. Like most kids, he had no problem adjusting to the tones. (Kids are "in the moment," eager to learn.) Within minutes he was swinging at 28/11, and his clubhead speed jumped from 67 to 77 miles per hour. That translated into an instant gain of 20 yards with his 5-iron.

Josh Weems, Before & After 30-Minute Tempo Training Session

	Average Clubhead Speed at Impact		Estimated Carry		Frames Ratio		Total Elapsed Time in Seconds	
	Before	After	Before	After	Before	After	Before	After
5-iron	67 MPH	77 MPH	124	144	39/11	28/11	1.67	1.30
Driver	---	---	---	---	---	---	---	---

Follow-Up: A year after his tempo training, Josh was shooting in the middle to high 70s for eighteen holes, playing from the front tees. This summer Josh shot a career-best 73, and had several subpar 9-hole rounds at his home course.

CASE STUDY 44-09

Name: Wint Winter, Jr.

Occupation: Lawyer and banker **Age:** 49

Handicap: Not established

Average Carry with Driver: 205 yards

Average Carry with 5-iron: 150 yards

Self-Evaluation: "I took up golf last year because I need to learn how to accept frustration in my life. This is a game with a lot of moving parts to it, and it's all foreign to me. I know I need to work on being more relaxed. In high school I broke the state record for the discus throw in practice, but I never did it in meets because of tension. Golf is hard because when I'm over the ball I have to think about ten different things."

Trainer: John Novosel, Jr.

Training Site: Lawrence Country Club, Lawrence, Kansas

Test Swings (3 representative swings)

	Clubhead Speed at Impact			Frames Ratio			Total Elapsed Time in Seconds		
	Swing 1	Swing 2	Swing 3	Swing 1	Swing 2	Swing 3	Swing 1	Swing 2	Swing 3
5-iron	78 MPH	79 MPH	85 MPH	27/10	26/10	26/10	1.23	1.20	1.20
Driver	89 MPH	87 MPH	90 MPH	27/8	27/8	28/8	1.17	1.17	1.20

Diagnosis: Wint is an accomplished athlete and a competitor—he was a football center at the University of Kansas and then a state legislator—but everything about golf is new to him. When I asked him about his tempo, he said, "Tempo? I've heard the word." His golf swing is quite good for a new player, but his self-diagnosis is right on the mark—he has too much tension in his arms and shoulders at address. He also has a grip that's way too weak. Most of his misses are thin shots to the right; he has a tendency to push the ball with an open clubface and fall back. On the other hand, some of Wint's test swings are close to the Tour Tempo model—25/8 with the 5-iron, 27/8 with the driver. If he strengthens his grip, rids himself of tension, and practices the Tour Tempo Workout, he should see significant improvement.

Training Report: I started Wint with the 5-iron and the 24/8 Tour Tempo tape. Since he was already swinging at a brisk tempo, I skipped the preset drill and let him take practice swings to the tones from a normal address position, just brushing the grass. When he started hitting balls, we saw no immediate increase in clubhead speed and his shots continued to go right. Convinced that his weak grip was the problem, I had him move his left hand a little more on top of the club and then, with the headphones off, put him through a few minutes of Y and L drills.

When he put the headphones back on and resumed hitting his 5-iron to the tones, we saw an immediate change. His very first shot was a long pull-draw. His next shot was a straight draw that flew even farther. "What happened there?" Wint asked. (Answer: With his grip strengthened, the toe of Wint's club was now pointing *up* after impact. Before, his clubface was facing the sky.) For the next ten minutes Wint hit the ball solidly and straight, and every shot had a slight draw. His clubhead speed gradually increased, too, inching up to 93 or 94 miles per hour. That translated to about 15 more yards of carry on every shot.

When he switched to the driver, Wint's draw disappeared and he hit everything to the right again. "Mentally tired?" he wondered aloud. Probably. But I also noticed that his grip had slipped back into its weak position. I had him hit some more 5-irons to the 24/8 tape so he would end the session on a high note. Which he did. "I've never hit an iron that far," he said afterward. "I've never been able to hit my irons at all." Asked what the difference was, Wint said, "All I had to focus on was the tempo. It's making me not think about those ten things."

Analysis of Wint's tape showed that Tour Tempo had shortened his backswing slightly, saving a frame or two per swing. He was a consistent 24/8 or 25/8, and that's about as good as you can get.

Wint Winter, Before & After 30-Minute Tour Tempo Session

	Average Clubhead Speed at Impact		Estimated Carry		Frames Ratio		Total Elapsed Time in Seconds	
	Before	After	Before	After	Before	After	Before	After
5-iron	81 MPH	90 MPH	152	169	26/10	23/8	1.20	1.03
Driver	89 MPH	88 MPH	205.6	203.3	27/8	24/8	1.17	1.07

Follow-Up: Wint significantly improved his balance and increased his clubhead speed by 9 miles per hour, which enabled him to add 18 yards carry to every club in his bag. His shot pattern is so much better now that his golfing friends have remarked on his improvement. He'll need to utilize the Tour Tempo Workout to continue the improvement of his swing. "I have played a couple of times," Wint reported in an e-mail, "and find my stroke to be very much improved."

"It's what you learn after you know it all that counts."

John Wooden

11

John Novosel's Little Red Book

"I prefer to teach with images, parables and metaphors," Harvey Penick wrote in the introduction to his 1992 best-seller, Harvey Penick's Little Red Book. *For sixty years the teaching pro from Austin, Texas, scribbled his notes and observations into a red notebook, which he kept locked in a briefcase. With the help of Texas writer Bud Shrake, he turned it into a neat compendium of bite-sized golf wisdom—some of which, admittedly, conflicts with what I've learned through my tempo studies. Some of his observations, though, could be pasted right into this book. He writes, "People talk about the 'relaxed' swing of Bobby Jones. But look at a photograph of Bobby's face at impact. You can see the frown of intense effort and concentration."*

I love that.

Anyway, Penick's literary method is the inspiration for the following musings.

The Link

Having looked at hundreds of golf swings through the microscope of tempo analysis, I am sure of one thing: Mechanics and tempo are linked. It is virtually impossible to repeat a mechanically sound swing if your timing is irregular. Similarly, you can't have consistent tempo if you are casting, swaying, making a reverse pivot, or rerouting the golf club. As my son John, Jr. likes to say, "You can't pick up one end of a stick without picking up the other."

Perfecting one's tempo, however, produces quicker and better results than trying to fix a swing flaw. The tour pro's slight rerouting of the club, too minor to pick up with the naked eye, is difficult to correct with traditional methods. (Who has a drill to correct a three-quarter-inch deflection of the shaft on the downswing?) It is easier, by far, to iron out swing wrinkles with tempo training.

Take the hypothetical example of Player X, a touring pro with a tempo ratio of 24/8. If X records a video of his ailing swing and finds that he is swinging at 26/9, it becomes a simple game of "Where did the time go?" Somewhere on that video, X is going to find three frames of "dithering"—an unnecessary pause, a wandering off plane, a hitch, a downcock, whatever. Armed with this knowledge, X can either embark on a complicated correction program with his swing guru . . . or he can simply slip on his headphones and retrain his swing to the beeps and chirps of the 24/8 Tour Tempo track.

Wrinkles out, instantly.

Paralysis by Analysis

A while back I bought a used book that describes the swing thoughts of various players and teachers. (I collect most anything that has to do with golf instruction.) When the book came, I thumbed through it eagerly. In the back, one of the book's owners had written down thirteen different things to focus on as he performed the golf swing.

Thirteen!

Not that you need to buy a book to load up on swing thoughts. Here are some tidbits I picked up from recent issues of *Golf Digest* and *GOLF Magazine.*

"For more power, lead with your left hand."

"You must take the clubhead straight back, *slowly* and low to the ground."

"For more power, hit the ball with your right hand."

And how about this one? "During the backswing, the outside of the left foot should rise slightly off the ground, but the inside of the foot, from toe to heel, should remain planted. When the left foot rolls in this manner from a slightly flared position at address, the left knee will move laterally toward the right knee and, more importantly, the clubhead will remain on the correct swing plane."

Most of us spend our whole lives trying to learn the golf swing from these outdated and unworkable methods. As Joel Barker has written, "When in the middle of the paradigm, it is hard to imagine any other paradigm."

Who Has the Best Tempo?

Ernie Els? Nick Faldo? Tiger Woods?

It's a question you hear a lot when tour players gather. "I love to watch Fred Couples," one pro says. "He's so smooth, everything looks effortless." Another pro casts his vote for David Toms. "He's a wonderful ball-striker, and nobody hits fairway woods better. That's a sure sign of good tempo."

The irony, of course, is that all the above-mentioned touring pros have the same tempo—that is, they all exhibit the same 3-to-1 ratio of backswing to forward swing. When tour players say someone's tempo is the best, they mean that player's timing is the most *consistent.* Repeatability is the key to success on the PGA Tour, where just one ragged swing can result in a loss of tens or even hundreds of thousands of dollars.

So again, who's got the best tempo? Which touring pro can count on his inner clock to function flawlessly over four rounds of tournament golf?

One way to answer that question is to videotape the pros under tournament conditions and then check for variability in their swing times. I have done this often over the last two years, so I can say with reasonable certainty that the pro with the most perfect timing is (drum roll) . . . Tiger Woods.

Okay, no surprise there. The interesting thing about Woods, as noted earlier, is that he has speeded up his tempo in recent years while maintaining the critical 3-to-1 ratio. When I first timed him, using tape from the 1997 Masters, he was a consistent 27/9. These days, with a swing revamped by teaching pro Butch Harmon, Tiger is a steady 24/8.

I collected some great data on Woods when he won the 2002 U.S. Open. Before the final round, NBC showed him warming up on the range at Bethpage Black. Tiger had his Sunday red shirt on and a couple of wire baskets of balls at his feet. He warmed up with a few short pitch shots, taking a smooth half-swing. I timed those swings at 24/9. He then hit several wedges while applying cut spin; the ball probably wasn't flying more than 40 or 50 yards. Those swings timed at 24/10. Every one of Tiger's backswings took an identical 24 frames.

When he started hitting full shots, Tiger's downswing speeded up to 8 frames, but his backswing stayed at 24. It didn't matter if he was taking a half-swing, a three-quarter swing, or a full swing—*every single backswing timed out at 24 frames.*

The real test, of course, is what happens on the golf course under tournament pressure. Woods had a two-stroke lead over Sergio Garcia when he teed off. Tiger's 3-wood tee shot hit the first fairway, leaving him 126 yards to the hole. His approach shot with a wedge found the middle of the green. Both shots, when timed on the computer, were exactly 24/8.

At that point I was pretty sure that Woods was going to win his eighth major championship. His inner clock, his unparalleled sense of timing, had him swinging with perfect rhythm, shot . . . after shot . . . after shot.

Launch Angle

Fred Shoemaker frees up his ball-bound students by having them literally throw their golf clubs, but I don't recommend this type of training, unless you are under the direct supervision of Fred. I tried it once in 1986, before Fred's book, with John, Jr. at an open field near our house. Junior released his club a little late. Instead of going straight, it spun end over end and flew right over the top of our van.

Junior was embarrassed. He said, "I guess there's a reason why they have cages around guys who throw the hammer."

Where *Does* the Time Go?

Even the best players make shaky swings. One of the players I analyzed at Bethpage Black was Ernie Els, who, a month later, would win the British Open at Muirfield. On the 205-yard third hole, Els pulled his tee shot into a greenside bunker. When I timed that swing, I found that he had missed his usual 24/8 tempo by several frames. He had swung, instead, at 23/10. One frame difference in total elapsed time isn't much, but the distribution of those frames was odd. Els's backswing was only 1 frame fast—within the margin of measurement error—but his downswing was 2 frames slow.

Or was it? When I looked at the swing again in stop-motion, focusing on his hand action, I saw that Els had put the club in perfect position at the top. But then his hands had moved laterally instead of starting right back down. That little wandering of the club used up almost 2 frames of time and threw his swing off enough to spoil the shot.

I found a more pronounced tendency to dither at the top in Nick

Faldo. When Faldo completed his backswing, he let the shaft fall slightly behind him before starting down. Put another way, he "flattened" his swing plane. A golfer of Faldo's stature might be doing that intentionally, if he thinks his swing is too upright. But any significant deflection from the original swing plane tends to be a tempo killer. (Faldo's approach shot to the first hole landed short and rolled back toward the fairway, causing him to glare in disbelief.) Phil Mickelson, when we taped his swing a few years ago, used to be loose like that at the top, and it made him very inconsistent. He has since tightened up his swing considerably, but when Phil hits a wild, off-tempo shot, as he did often in 2003, you still see some rerouting at the top.

A couple of months later, when I analyzed tape of Faldo playing in a European Tour event, his little dither at the top was gone and his tempo was back to a 20/8.

"Smooth"

The best one-word swing thought ever devised.

The mechanically sound swing is smooth because it is free of jerky detours, loops, and lunges. The properly timed swing is smooth for exactly the same reason—the club is delivered to the ball in the most time-efficient manner.

The best pro swings are marvels of biomechanical efficiency. Ireland's Padraig Harrington, a two-time Ryder Cupper, has a perfect transition from backswing to forward swing. His hands and club stop at the top and start back down on the same path without delay. The swing of PGA Tour veteran Jeff Maggert is similarly free of wasted motion.

Of course, nobody has a smoother transition than Tiger Woods. I have studied hundreds of his swings, and 95 times out of 100 his club changes direction with no deflection of the hands or shaft.

That's smooth.

Send in the Clones

In 1988, I attended a five-day session of the Jack Nicklaus Golf Academy at the Grand Cypress Resort in Orlando, Florida. I was one of ten students, and every morning we beat balls for three hours.

One by one they took us aside for a computer swing analysis. Someone had taken seventy touring pros, mapped their swings with a computer, and created a composite stick figure with the "perfect" golf swing. Then, for purposes of comparison, they put this perfect swing side-by-side with a stick-figure rendering of the student's swing.

I thought it was great. One of the best teaching tools I had ever seen.

The problem was, after looking at your tape and pointing out where your swing was deficient, they sent you back to the tee to beat more balls while trying to achieve those perfect swing positions. They said nothing about tempo. The data was right there in the computer, but conventional wisdom said that good tempo and good mechanics were two different cats.

I'm sure if I had asked the instructors why it was good to copy the *positions* but not the *timing* of the perfect swing, they would have patiently explained that everyone has their own natural tempo and it is no use copying someone else's. Some people walk fast, some people talk fast, blah, blah, blah.

They didn't know any better. But, to be fair, neither did I.

The Reflexive Swing

Conventional golf wisdom has you taking a "tip" and going to the range. You then try to hit balls while thinking of this tip.

Tour Tempo requires a different mind-set. With Tour Tempo you use conscious thought to control your swing only at the beginning of the program.

You learn the golf swing through the Tour Tempo Workout. This is similar to the way you learned typing. At first you performed drills in groups or clusters to associate pressing a key with a letter of the alphabet. Once you had "keyed" these into your memory, you started hitting the correct key without thinking about it. All you have to do now is think of the words, and your fingers automatically hit the right keys.

This is how the golf swing should be learned—by *feel*, with just the right amount of intellectual involvement.

Distance Improves Accuracy

All golfers know that it is easier to hit a 9-iron straight than it is to hit a driver straight. That's because the higher the loft of the club, the more backspin it puts on the ball. Your driver, for example, puts about 60 revolutions per second on the ball, while your 9-iron produces about 130 revolutions per second. Backspin is what keeps the ball in the air longer and makes it fly straighter. The less-lofted the clubface, the more sidespin it puts on the ball on unsquare hits. Sidespin makes the ball curve right or left.

That's the scientific explanation for the clear correlation between driving distance and greens hit in regulation. Picture a 400-yard par-4. If your clubhead speed with the driver is 95 miles per hour and you hit your drive 220 yards, you're left with a 3-iron into the green. But if your clubhead speed is 15 miles per hour faster (thanks to Tour Tempo), your drive will go 254 yards, leaving only a 9-iron to the green.

How many more greens would you hit if you had a 9-iron in your hand instead of a 3-iron?

Tour Tempo Lite

I let some friends read the *Tour Tempo* manuscript before publication to make sure it was clear and understandable. A few told me they were already practicing Tour Tempo. "I tried swinging faster a few years ago," one said, "and since then I've played much better." Another said he had tried swinging to music, "but I didn't see any improvement, so I stopped."

Others, hearing me talk about Tour Tempo, say they have already tried it. When I ask what they mean, they say that they have swung to a metronome or the sound of the ocean surf.

Listen, folks. Those things may be pleasant. They may even be helpful (by quieting the conscious mind). But until you practice to the Tour Tempo audio tracks, you haven't tried Tour Tempo. The best golfers in the world swing with a specific 3-to-1 tempo, and it has nothing to do with metronomes, the waltz, or tribal chants.

It's more like chemistry. Just as you need two hydrogen atoms for every oxygen atom to make water, you need three units of backswing to every unit of forward swing to create Tour Tempo.

Close only counts in horseshoes.

Appendix A

Three "Mats Only" Internet Columns by Sports Illustrated *Senior Writer John Garrity*

May 23, 2001

A Lesson in Tempo

SOUTHERN PINES, NC—I played Pinehurst No. 2 yesterday morning with the course superintendent, two golf architects . . . and better tempo. In fact, any objective observers would have told you that my swing reminded them of "Mr. 59," Al Geiberger—a player whose pass at the ball was regarded as so smooth by his PGA Tour peers that he wound up on the SyberVision golf tapes.

Knowing that this claim will be met with skepticism, I invite those of you with broad-band modems to check out the accompanying video. For the rest of you, who get by with coal-powered Internet service, I'll describe what's on this remarkable video: Two driver swings, side by side—mine, recorded a few weeks ago in a backyard in Leawood, Kansas, and Geiberger's, filmed on June 10, 1977, the day he shot 59 at the Danny Thomas Memphis Classic. (Check out the groovy pants.) The takeaway of our swings has been synchronized; the result is a display of tandem grace and power rarely seen outside an Olympic venue. My swing tempo and Geiberger's are virtually identical through impact.

Watch again, this time in slow-motion. From takeaway to the top and back again to impact, Geiberger and I look like we're being controlled by the same servo-mechanism. The swings don't part company until the follow-through—and that happens only because Geiberger is hitting a golf ball with a driver and I'm hitting a tiny pup-tent with a Velcro-covered sphere glued to the end of a driver shaft.

Not to sound like an infomercial, but *I achieved this miraculous result in one thirty-minute lesson! And I did it without the aid of hypnosis, electrical stimulation, or mind-altering drugs!* All I did was spend a couple of hours with John Novosel, the Leawood businessman and golf gadfly. This is the guy, you may remember, who finagled his way into Mats Only a few months ago by buying me lunch and boasting that he had discovered how to teach the tempo secrets of the touring pros. (He didn't actually boast, but he did buy me lunch.) "I just need a couple of hours of your time," he told me. "I'll record your swing and analyze it on the computer. Then I'll show you some things that I think will interest you."

Fast-forward to a recent morning. The place: the Robin Nigro Golf Academy & Practice Center in Kansas City, Mo. I was hitting balls off a mat when John arrived with his digital Minicam and his "Swing-Mate®," a little box that measures clubhead speed. First he videoed my 5-iron swing. I hit the ball pretty well, and the digital readout on the little box read "96." John put down his camera and showed me a chart full of numbers. According to the chart, a 5-iron clubhead moving at 96 miles per hour will fly the ball 180 yards—assuming that the clubface meets the ball squarely.

John then had me hit a few balls with my driver. I hit these balls very well. (I was in one of those two-week spells where my timing was good enough to put the ball in the fairway half the time.) My clubhead speed with the driver was 110 miles per hour, which translated to a ball flight of 254 yards—"PGA" distance, according to the chart.

When John was satisfied that the swings he had recorded were representative, we went to his house, which is just off a fairway at the Leawood South Country Club. He pulled a chair up to a table in his breakfast room, fired up his Macintosh PowerBook, and then downloaded my swings from the camera to the computer, using a version of Final Cut Pro software. I realized right off that he was not exactly Steven Spielberg; he had shot my driver swing with a roof support blocking the camera. But hey, this is Mats Only, not the U.S.C. Film School.

John then went into this mad scientist routine—slowing the swings down, muttering to himself, writing numbers in a notebook. "Your swing mechanics look pretty solid," he said at last. "Your position at impact is good. I do notice a little casting at the top." He moved the image forward and back, forward and back. I saw my wrists breaking down, the clubhead dipping toward the ground.

"Sometimes the clubhead drops into my peripheral vision," I said. "It's startling."

"But take a look at this. Between the time you start that casting motion and the time the clubhead reaches the ball, you make some sort of correction. Your position is good at impact. To be honest, there are good players, tour-quality players, who do the same thing. However . . ."

He didn't have to complete the thought. Corrections of that sort require constant practice to time correctly.

"Anyway," he said, "you're a . . ." And he gave me two numbers.

I have to be coy about this, because Novosel and his collaborators (including *Golf Magazine* Top 100 teaching pros John Rhodes and Gerald McCullagh) are in the swing-aid business. But here's the essence of what he told me: Despite being told for years that I had a tendency to be "too quick" and should "slow down, keep it smooth" . . . I was, in fact, taking the club back too *slowly.* (If you compare my "before" swing to Geiberger's swing, you'll see that Geiberger hits the ball before I even complete my backswing.) What's more, most amateurs do the same thing. We all follow the old Bobby Jones dictum, "Nobody ever swung a golf club too slowly"—which probably made a lot of sense in the age of hickory shafts, but is bunk in the era of Tiger Woods. "Everybody teaches 'low and slow,'" John said, "but the tour pros just don't do this. They are much quicker on the backswing than they look."

He got up from the table. "Now we go outside and I show you how to swing the club with the tempo of Tiger Woods and Phil Mickelson." John went into an adjoining room and started rummaging through an assortment of golf clubs and odd-looking shafts . . .

Oh, hell, look at the time. I have to run out to Pine Needles and get ready for the U.S. Women's Open. I'll continue this tale of tempo—or, as John calls it in his promotional literature, "Golf's Last Secret Finally Revealed!"—in my next column.

You *can* keep a secret, can't you?

June 14, 2001

Tempo Produces Technique

TULSA, OK—Before I so rudely interrupted myself, I was relating how I got my swing smoothed out by John Novosel, the tempo titan of Leawood, Kansas. We were in his breakfast room, remember? Sun streaming in the garden window . . .

"I really like your swing," John told me, looking at the video of my swing that he had downloaded on his laptop. "I think the only thing you need is the tempo. You aren't getting everything out of your swing that you could."

Having concluded that my backswing was too slow, John asked me to step into his backyard for an instant cure. This time I swung with an XLR8R® club. (Pronounce it "accelerator.") The XLR8R® was co-designed by John Rhodes, a well-known teaching pro who has worked with Tom Kite, Curtis Strange, Hal Sutton, and other PGA Tour pros. It substitutes Velcro-to-Velcro contact for club-to-ball contact and sounds like you're cracking a whip when you make contact. But it lets you work on your impact position without worrying about ball flight.

Anyway, John put me through about ten minutes of a drill designed to match my tempo to that of a successful touring pro—say, Phil Mickelson. "You've got to be kidding," I said. My swings, when I followed his directions, felt short and impossibly fast. "Man!" I laughed and shook my head. "I feel like I'm yanking hot toast out of a toaster."

"Wait until you see this video." He was looking through the eyepiece of his Minicam. "You won't believe it."

There was a short delay when I accidentally whacked the impact target into a tree, but I practiced my swing-on-speed until John was satisfied. We then went back into the house, and he downloaded the new video onto his PowerBook.

"Aha!" He began to laugh. "This is awesome. This gives me chills." He turned the computer toward me and beamed. "How good is that?"

I looked at my driver swing, and my jaw dropped. (It didn't actually drop. That's just a way of saying I was astonished.) Not only did my swing not look hurried. It looked *smoother.* And not only did it look smoother, my chronic swing mistakes had vanished. That little casting action at the top, which I've had since I went to two golf schools for a *Sports Illustrated* story in 1989—*gone.* That nasty habit of hanging back on my right side through impact—*gone.* That tendency to search my pockets for cash while somebody else pays for the sandwiches and drinks—okay, tempo doesn't cure everything. But I had to agree with John: Matching my swing tempo to that of the Tour players had fixed certain faults without any conscious effort on my part.

"I think tempo and mechanics are married," John said. "Your cast is gone because casting is actually a function of taking it back too slow." (My dad used to have a contemptuous name for that breaking of the wrists at the top. He called it "the old dipsy-doo.")

"By speeding up," I said, "I don't really have time to cast. The swing feels more reflexive. It's less a collection of conscious body movements."

John nodded with a big smile that said *exactly.* "If you look at

Tiger's swing, his club doesn't wander. He doesn't need to re-route it from the top. He doesn't waste precious time or clubhead speed."

I studied my swing as John played it over and over again on his laptop. I really liked what I saw. "I've always thought that good tempo was a natural consequence of good technique and hard work. You practice long enough, you get smooth." John was still smiling, so I finished the thought. "This suggests that proper tempo produces proper technique."

"I think it does." He quickly added, "I don't want to claim too much. A golfer with bad fundamentals won't get the immediate results you got. But we have two little swinging drills that go with the tempo package, and they take care of swing plane, squaring the club at impact—all the mechanical stuff that has to be mastered." He tapped on his touchpad, and Al Geiberger's swing appeared again on the screen (a good swing, but not quite in a class with mine). "To be honest," John said, "I was a bit nervous trying this with you. If it hadn't worked, I knew I'd look like a real jackass in Mats Only."

"Not to worry," I said. "I'm the only jackass in Mats Only."

When I left John Novosel's house a few minutes later, I had my arms full of his gadgets—two XLR8R® "striking clubs," a collapsible impact target, a small rubber mat, a couple of "resistance aprons" (for the impact target, not for me), a Walkman-type cassette player, portable earphones, a tape, and a training manual called *TourProTempo: Golf's Last Secret Finally Revealed.*

I headed for the range.

July 4, 2001

New King of Swing

KANSAS CITY, MO—I didn't have to go out for fireworks tonight. I just opened the Mats Only mailbag.

"Garrity, you bastard!" begins an e-mail from a reader who identifies himself only as "August O'Meara" of Minneapolis, Minnesota. "Thanks so very much for leaving us hanging. I have to WASTE another week hacking it around, while you know the secret to making a perfect tempo swing." (O'Meara is referring, of course, to two recent Mats Only columns which feature "before and after" videos—one of my best driving range swings followed by the same swing under the influence of tempo coach John Novosel.) "The two videos are night and day, for God's sake. The before swing, are you even swinging? Then the after swing—a miracle caught on film! Absolutely the same pace as Geiberger's swing, from takeaway to follow-through. Amazing. How long did it take to learn that tempo?"

Answer: About as long as it took you to write your e-mail. The second video was made about 90 minutes after the first, with most of that time taken up by the drive to Novosel's house, watching him mumble over his laptop, etc. The swing drill itself took about 10 minutes.

Jack Feldman of Los Angeles submits this more skeptical message: "All well and good that your swing looks better hitting a Velcro towel. I haven't missed a two-footer on my carpet in years, but it's something else on the golf course. What happens when you hit a golf ball?" In a similar vein, Jay Morran, also of L.A., writes, "I can't believe you get 10 days to write such a short and silly article. Not that I didn't enjoy it, but come on! Tempo is very important, yet hitting the ball is what matters. Tell us how well your new, non-Velcro tempo worked on the course."

Fair question, guys. I've only played three rounds since my session with Novosel. In May I played Colbert Hills, the new Kansas State University layout in Manhattan, Kansas. I didn't keep score, but I remember about 13 pars, and I kinda liked my drive on the par-5 first hole, which sailed downhill and downwind about 365 yards. I would guess I shot around 80. The week of the U.S. Women's Open I played Pinehurst No. 2 with golf architects Bobby Weed and Scot Sherman and No. 2's course superintendent, Paul Jett. We played from the blue tees, and I shot about 81, finishing with the ball I started with. (I say "about 81" because I picked up on the par-3 17th when I was out of the hole. Give me a double-bogey.) I 3-putted four or five times on Donald Ross's tricky greens and missed three or four good birdie opportunities.

My other outing, the week of the U.S. Open, was at the notoriously difficult Oak Tree Golf Club in Edmund, Oklahoma, site of the 1988 PGA Championship. I played maybe 23 holes over two days, from the members' tees, and if you take any 18 holes as a round, I broke 80. (Two birdies.) I'm not talking senior tour here, but all three rounds were better than the crappy play I usually report in this column—as regular readers can attest.

But then, I may be kidding myself. Or so Joe Davis of Millburn, New Jersey, would have me believe. "Quite frankly, old chap, I detect a bit of wishful thinking here. In fact, there's no great similarity between your swing and Al Geiberger's. Al's swing is a thing of beauty, a classic wedding of function and form, while your swing is rather ordinary. Granted, the timing is similar, but the mechanics are worlds apart.

"But don't despair," he continues, imagining my crestfallen reaction. "It's not a bad swing, and if you can score with it, great. Carry on!"

Joe, of course, is way off base. If you look at the two swings again, you'll see that Geiberger's swing looks so good because his pants look so bad. I, on the other hand—a famously snappy dresser—lose style points because I look so good *before* I take the club back.

A less judgmental correspondent, Chris Crowe of Richmond, Virginia, writes merely to ask a pertinent question: "When you say you are 'casting' at the top of the swing, what does that mean?"

Answer: "Casting" is just one term for the very common fault of losing your wrist angle. Most commonly it appears as excess wrist break at the top of the swing, which sends the clubhead plunging toward the ground before the start of the downswing. Most good players have little or no cast in their swings; it really screws up your timing.

Finally, a bunch of you hissed at me for not providing an address or a web link to John Novosel. Frankly, I didn't include it because I'm not a shill for John or for anybody else who has a swing aid or a miracle club to sell. Plus, I don't want you coming to me in five months saying, "I was a two handicap, but now, thanks to you, I'm swinging faster than Alvin and the Chipmunks."

But since you asked, I typed "xlr8r" in my search engine and got the web site for the XLR8R®, www.xlr8rgolf.com. According to the site, the XLR8R® is sold in kits ranging from $149.95 to $299.95, plus shipping and handling. Then I clicked on the "TourPro Tempo" button and read a letter that made me gulp. "This stuff is so new and revolutionary," the letter said, "that to take lessons from John you'll need to sign a nondisclosure agreement promising that you will not reveal the secrets that he discloses to you. He gives one-on-one personal lessons and needs you for two days at a time in Overland Park, Kansas, a suburb of Kansas City." And then the killer: "It's gonna cost you $5,000."

Full disclosure time, folks. I didn't pay a cent. And John paid for lunch at Hallbrook Country Club.

Still, if you're one of those lucky ones who cashed in his stock options before the market went south, you may consider $5,000 a small price to pay for a peek at the Rosetta Stone of golf. You can reach John at (888) 411-1989.

I, on the other hand, am going to go to the mirror and stare at my Novoseled swing. Apparently it's worth a whole lot of money.

Tour Tempo—Pro Impact—
Hands ahead of clubhead at impact

Amateur Impact—
Hands behind clubhead at impact

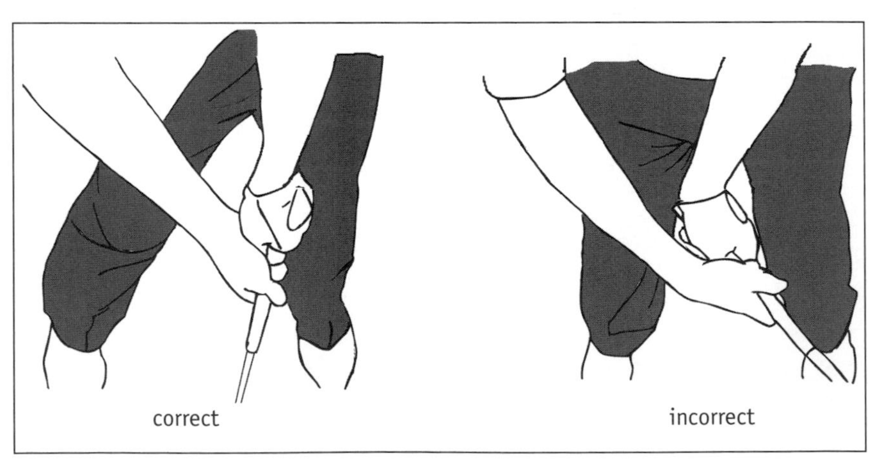

View from above

Appendix B

Curing the Over-the-Top, Casting, Chicken-Winging Move Made by 90 Percent of Golfers

The most surprising benefit of Tour Tempo training is the remarkable effect it has on the casting, wrist-flipping move that causes most of the really bad shots in golf. This move has various names—casting, cupping, releasing early, coming over the top, chicken-winging, etc. Over 90 percent of golfers suffer from the casting affliction. It is the source of your weak slice—or, depending on the alignment of the clubhead at impact, your strong pull-hook, your fat shot, and your topped shot.

What do we mean by casting? David Leadbetter describes it as an "early release . . . a 'scoopy' position [at impact] . . . the right hand wraps over the left as the left wrist collapses . . ." In anatomical terms, the left hand goes into dorsi flexion and the right hand goes into palmar extension.

Conventional Golf Wisdom teachers have historically defined casting by the "scoopy" position of the hands and wrists shown on the opposite page. There are actually two other important places in the swing where this can be detected. We'll explore them on the following pages.

Power angle at start of downswing

At the start of the downswing, the shaft of the club and the left arm represent an acute angle, the power angle. If, by the time the left arm gets to parallel in the downswing, that power angle has been lost, we say that the golfer has "cast" the club. The move is analogous to the wristy cast of the fly fisherman.

Why is this a problem? Because the power angle represents stored power in the golf swing. When it is released early and incorrectly, you lose clubhead speed. You also lose accuracy because casting makes it nearly impossible to keep the clubface square through impact.

Any good teaching pro can diagnose a caster simply by looking at his divots (or lack of them) and by observing his ball flight (the ball starts left and spins uncontrollably). The devilish details, however, are best understood by videotaping the swing and checking to see if the power angle has been retained at three key points.

Here's what a typical golfer's casting action looks like compared to our Tour Tempo models, at the three Key Points in the swing that define casting.

Key Point #1—Left arm parallel to ground on downswing:

Power angle retained

Power angle lost

Key Point #2—Relationship of the leading forearm to the club shaft as hands work their way back in front of the body:

Power angle retained

Power angle lost

Key Point #3—Relationship of the leading forearm to the club shaft, and the relationship of the hands to the ball at impact:

Power angle retained

Power angle lost

Compare this mid-handicapper's action at the three Key Points to that of a Tour Tempo model. Notice especially the difference between "Power angle lost" and "Power angle retained." Because casting adds loft to the clubhead, it turns a 5-iron into a 7-iron, robbing you of distance. You also lose accuracy, because casting causes all kinds of misalignments of the clubhead at impact and the relationship of the hands to the ball at impact.

Notice as well the difference in the overall motion of their bodies. The amateur in the photo sequence was clocked at 44/10, the pro at 24/8.

So how do you stop casting?

Well, you can try *holding* the power angle. Leadbetter recommends a couple of exercises that promote an awareness of what a desired "late hit" feels like. In the first exercise you grip the club crosshanded and try to maintain your wrist cock as long as you can on the downswing. In the second, you push the clubhead against the corner of a wall while simulating impact with your hands slightly ahead.

Unfortunately, making a conscious effort to control your wrists during an actual swing is extremely difficult. It increases tension in the arms and hands and often results in an open clubface, causing the mother of all slices. Furthermore, it doesn't help you *feel* what you are trying to accomplish. (The golfer's lament: "I know what I should be doing. I just can't do it.")

A more promising approach—but hardly foolproof—requires the expenditure of a few dollars for one of the commercially available swing aids that promise to cure casting. You no doubt remember "The Secret," that plastic-brace gizmo hawked in infomercials for a couple of years. The Secret buckled onto the back of your right wrist and kept it from breaking down through impact. That was fine, up to a point. The brace prevented scooping and promoted the proper lead-with-the-hands action on chip shots. But The Secret was flawed. For one thing, when swinging at full speed, it hurt; the inflexible plastic bruised the back of the hand. For another, it froze the wrong angle. (The key angle in the modern golf swing is actually the straight-line relationship of the club shaft to the left forearm.) The Secret, whatever its strengths, didn't cure the actual cause of the cast, which is the improper motion of the whole body.

> Clubhead lag (the power angle) is the "Secret of Golf." It is simple, elusive, indispensable, without substitute or compensation and always present.
>
> —Homer Kelly, *The Golfing Machine*

Another swing aid designed to prevent casting and the over-the-top move is the hinged club. The most heavily advertised of these, the Medicus, is designed to break down, or hinge, if you swing it off-plane. The Medicus unwittingly encourages a superslow (not Tour Tempo) takeaway as the golfer tries to keep the club from hinging.

For a high-tech solution to the casting problem you can try David

Leadbetter's LazerGuide. This device, which attaches to the grip of any golf club, fires a red laser beam out the bottom of the club. Swinging the club back in slow motion, you keep the laser beam pointed directly at a line on a swing-path mat, guaranteeing that your swing plane doesn't become too flat or too upright. The drawbacks: 1) The laser beam is hard to see outdoors and 2) disappears entirely when you swing at full speed.

For a low-tech attempt to solve the casting problem that doesn't work and is potentially dangerous, you can go to the hardware store and spend less than three dollars for a 1/16th-inch, three-foot metal rod. This rod, when inserted in the tiny hole in the end of any golf grip, extends off your left hip and forces you to swing with your hands leading the clubhead through impact. The drawbacks: 1) Like The Secret, the rod allows no release at all, making it easy to leave the clubface open on full shots. 2) It vibrates like a car antenna when it hits your hip. 3) It can raise a welt just above your belt line.

> Rhythm is the very soul of Golf.
>
> —Percy Boomer, *On Learning Golf*

If you've bought all these devices, and you're still casting—well, I'm not surprised. I judge any aid or instruction method by two criteria: 1) Does it minimize the casting action? 2) Does it encourage Tour Tempo timing in the swing? So far, nothing I've seen advertised on TV meets both criteria.

Why don't the swing aids work better? Because it's not your grip, your stance, or where your left elbow is pointing that makes you a caster. The most common cause of casting, I'm convinced, is improper tempo. (Casting is the logical consequence of taking the club back too slowly.) When our students incorporate Tour Tempo into their swings, they usually quit casting.

But a few don't.

So let's be clear about casting and your golf swing. You can actually play pretty good golf while casting. (When I was young and strong, I achieved a six-handicap, and I cast all the time.) On the other hand, there are four good reasons why you should go all-out to rid yourself of this habit:

1. If you keep casting, your swing speed will probably vary by plus-or-minus 10 miles per hour. This means shots with the same club will carry from 10 to 20 yards shorter or farther than you intend.
2. If you keep casting, you'll continue to see your good rounds destroyed by one or two "blow-up" holes.
3. If you keep casting, you'll never be able to take your range swing to the course. (On the range you usually hit one club over and over again from a level lie. The golf course doesn't grant you that luxury.)
4. If you keep casting, you will never hit the ball as far as you should—and it will only get worse as you age.

I repeat: To minimize the effects of casting, you must incorporate the Tour Tempo philosophy into your swing. (You'll find additional information about how to rid yourself of the casting motion on our website, www.tourtempo.com.) Proper tempo is not something to worry about next week or next year or whenever you think you'll be finished working on your swing.

Tour Tempo is a *fundamental.*

Appendix C

Using the Tour Tempo CD

Thank you for buying *Tour Tempo: Golf's Last Secret Finally Revealed.* The Tour Tempo CD, which accompanies the book, has both audio and video selections that review the Tour Tempo theory and provide you with the tools to set your own swing clock.

Video Files

The best place to start is with the introductory videos, which can be viewed on your PC or MAC computer:

1. **Tour Tempo Introduction.** This video explains the basics of the Tour Tempo Program.

2. **Tour Tempo Testing.** This video reviews the Tour Tempo testing protocol.

3. **Tour Tempo Workout.** This video shows you how to integrate Tour Tempo into your golf game.

These videos are best viewed in a window about the size of your palm. In Quicktime video you can advance frames one at a time by hitting the arrow keys on your keyboard. The latest version of Quicktime Player from Apple is helpful to play the videos. It can be downloaded free from http://www.apple.com/quicktime/download/.

Files 4 through 12 contain videos from the Case Studies (Chapter 10 in the book), are arranged by name:

4. **Bruce Provo**

5. **John Ross**

6. **Josh Weems**

7. **Greg Windholz**

8. **Tucker Weems**

9. **Bob Walsh**

10. **Collin Weems**

11. **Wint Winter**

12. **Betsy Provo**

Audio Files

The audio tracks, which you will use to teach yourself how to swing with the tempo ratio employed by the touring pros, are playable on any CD player (for practice in your living room or on the driving range with headphones). Tracks are provided for each of the three principal frame ratios—21/7, 24/8, and 27/9. (There are also two "hot tub" ratios, 30/10 and 33/11, which can be used to gradually adjust to the main Tour Tempo Tones, and also to maintain proper tempo while drilling on swing fundamentals.)

Each ratio has three audio tracks. The first is the **Swing-Set**, which teaches you the tempo of the backswing. Once you are comfortable with the first aspect of Tour Tempo (from takeaway to the top of the backswing), you can progress to the **Tempo Tones** and the **Swing-Set-Thru** voice prompts. Instructions for using the Tempo Tones are provided in Chapters 6 and 7. The voice prompts have been added because some golfers find them easier to use than the tones. When you hear the word "Swing," start the club back. "Set" is your signal to simultaneously set the wrists and start the forward swing. The word "Thru" should be timed to coincide with impact.

Audio Contents:

21/7—Swing Set
21/7—Pre-Shot
21/7—Pre-Shot Voice

24/8—Swing Set
24/8—Pre-Shot
24/8—Pre-Shot Voice

27/9—Swing Set
27/9—Pre-Shot
27/9—Pre-Shot Voice

30/10—Pre-Shot

33/11—Pre-Shot

The final audio selection, **Tour Tempo Golf Songs**, is a sample track from the Tour Tempo Tracks CD. The three-note guitar motif is synchronized to the 27/9 Tour Tempo ratio. You can listen to the song tracks on the course, at your computer, or even while driving in traffic. It's an effortless way to program your inner clock and improve your game.

We wish you luck (and longer shots and lower scores) using the Tour Tempo system.

Acknowledgments

There would be no Tour Tempo program without the patience and understanding of my wonderful wife, Mary Ann. Thanks, dear.

Thanks as well to my sons, Scott, Jeff, and John, Jr., three excellent athletes of whom I am very proud. Our mutual quest for the Holy Grail of golf—a repeatable and powerful swing—inspired the sixteen years of research that led to this book. The boys came up with many valuable insights, served as experimental guinea pigs, and even performed as models for illustrations and videos. Well done, guys.

My love of books and learning and my respect for the truth are a gift from my mother, Mary. My competitive spirit and love of athletics I inherited from my father, John. For sibling encouragement I have my sister, Judy, who also helped with the prototyping of several of my golf inventions. I owe a great deal to my extended family (aunts, uncles, and cousins) and to all those teachers and coaches whose positive influence has meant so much to me.

Tour Tempo, the book, owes its existence to an even larger cast. I would like to start by thanking my co-author, John Garrity, for translating my research into a readable and enjoyable book. (When I read some of John's passages for the first time, I felt like Robert DeNiro's character in *Analyze This,* who tells Billy Crystal, "You're good. You're *really* good.") Also indispensable was our agent, David McCormick, of

Collins & McCormick. David writes about golf himself and has edited virtually every top golf writer of our time.

My editor at Doubleday, Jason Kaufman, and his able assistant, Jenny Choi, gave me the no-doubt-false impression that book publishing is the most relaxed and nurturing industry in America. I also received incredible support from my own staff—Jeannie Padgett, Claudia Gloyd, Lori Eveler, and B. J. Smith—who "held down the fort" during those times that I had to be away from the office.

The Tour Tempo CD was an in-house production, but John and I got invaluable help in identifying and securing the rights to film clips of various golf stars and their beautiful swings. Special thanks to Shannon Doody and Marty Parks of the United States Golf Association and to Steve Robinson of CNN/SI, who helped us maneuver through a maze of licenses and permissions.

Finally, a parting salute to my golfing buddy and friend, Terry Huston, who helped us so much with all our projects, and to the rest of my golfing friends and to all the students who served as test subjects. Your well-timed efforts—and, in some cases, your poorly timed ones—made this book possible.

JOHN NOVOSEL is a businessman, inventor, and creator of the XLR8R® (pronounced "Accelerator"), a swing aid endorsed by many top golf coaches and used by numerous LPGA and PGA Tour golfers. He also has patents on three other golf training devices. Novosel is president of XLR8R, LLC, a golf training company. He gives tempo lessons and, with his sons, conducts golf schools in Overland Park, Kansas. If you would like to work with him, you can contact him through the Web site www.TourTempo.com.

JOHN GARRITY is a senior writer for *Sports Illustrated*, a columnist for Si.com, and author of more than a dozen books.